The USA Tax

The USA Tax

A Progressive Consumption Tax

Laurence S. Seidman

The MIT Press
Cambridge, Massachusetts
London, England

This book was set in Palatino by The MIT Press.
Printed and bound in the United States of America.

Library of Congress Cataloging-in-Publication Data

Seidman, Laurence S.
     The USA tax : a progressive consumption tax / Laurence S. Seidman.
        p.   cm.
     Includes bibliographical references and index.
     ISBN 0-262-19383-3 (hc : alk. paper)
        1. Spendings tax—United States.   2. Value-added tax—United States.   3. Taxation of articles of consumption—United States.   4. Income tax—United States.   I. Title.
     HJ5715.U6S45   1997
     336.2′7—dc21   96-41990
                                                                                        CIP

For my daughter Suzanna,
my son Jesse, and
my wife Ann.

Contents

Preface

This book is about the USA Tax, a tax bill introduced in the U.S. Congress in 1995 that represents a milestone in the story of the personal consumption tax that began a half century ago. But more fundamentally, this book is about the progressive personal consumption tax itself. The USA Tax comes closer to a progressive consumption tax than any tax bill ever introduced in Congress. Its central feature—the unlimited savings allowance—is true to the personal consumption tax ideal. In several important design details, however, the 1995 USA Tax bill strays from its ideal. A central theme of this book is that when the USA Tax goes astray, it gets into trouble as a consequence.

The subject of this book is a moving target (a specific tax bill in the U.S. Congress) and a fixed target (the progressive personal consumption tax). As this book goes to press in the fall of 1996, the 1995 bill still stands as introduced, though its designers are surely listening to suggestions for improvements. Some revisions may come about before you read this book; it is hoped that some changes will occur that will make certain criticisms obsolete. Any book that addresses evolving legislation faces the moving-target problem.

As you read this book, the USA Tax bill may be receiving a new burst of attention, or it may lie dormant in Congress. But whatever the short-term fate of the bill, this book focuses on the progressive personal consumption tax—a subject likely to endure. It has intrigued economists for half a century and engaged the efforts of numerous economists and tax specialists for the past two decades. This book tries to contribute to the theory and practical design of the progressive personal consumption tax.

I am indebted to the many authors whose work is cited throughout this book and to the designers of the 1995 USA Tax bill. I am especially grateful to the following individuals either for discussions concerning the personal consumption tax and/or the USA Tax, or for providing data for this book: Rudolph Penner, David Bradford, Lawrence Summers, Mervyn King, Frank Sammartino, Eric Toder, Denise Ramonas, Debra Miller, Barry Rogstad, Ernest Christian, William Hoagland, Peter Taylor, Rocky Rief, and Marcia Neilson-McPherson. My debt is greatest to my research partner, Kenneth Lewis.

1   The USA Tax

What is the USA (Unlimited Savings Allowance) Tax, what do its advocates claim it will accomplish, and why do they favor it over rival taxes? The introduction of the USA Tax bill into the United States Senate in April 1995, under the sponsorship of senators Pete Domenici (R-New Mexico), Sam Nunn (D-Georgia), and Bob Kerrey (D-Nebraska), represents an important milestone. The concept behind the USA Tax has been evolving for half a century (see this chapter's appendix), and the details of the USA Tax are still evolving. Virtually all USA Tax proponents agree on its core features, but several practical options are being modified in response to feedback and discussion. For example, Senator Domenici's detailed 1994 article does not always recommend the same treatment of these options as the April 1995 bill (hereafter referred to as "the 1995 bill") or the companion March 10, 1995, detailed explanation in *Tax Notes* authored by Ernest Christian and George Schutzer (hereafter referred to as "the 1995 explanation"). These practical options are discussed in chapter 4. This chapter focuses on the core features of the USA Tax.

The USA Tax has two components. Its household component takes as its ideal the progressive personal consumption tax. Its business component takes as its ideal the consumption-type, subtraction value-added tax (VAT). The version of the USA Tax presented in the 1995 bill diverges from these ideals in certain respects, but these details may change as the USA Tax provokes feedback and criticism. To understand the USA Tax, it is therefore necessary to understand the progressive personal consumption tax, and the consumption-type, subtraction VAT.

According to proponents, the aim of the USA Tax is to promote saving and investment while preserving the current distribution of the tax burden among income classes. To do this, the household component of the USA Tax uses a set of bracket tax rates that rise significantly as household consumption rises. USA Tax advocates claim that each rival tax either discourages saving and investment or shifts the distribution of the tax burden from the affluent to the nonaffluent. Advocates argue that the current income tax and the comprehensive (ideal) income tax discourage saving and investment; and that the national sales tax, value-added tax, and flat tax all promote saving and investment but shift the distribution of the tax burden from the affluent to the nonaffluent.

This book presents an explanation and analysis of the USA Tax and of the two ideals on which it is constructed: the progressive personal consumption tax, and the consumption-type, subtraction value-added tax. The book considers the arguments of advocates of the progressive personal consumption tax and the subtraction VAT, the replies of supporters of rival taxes, and the criticisms of tax experts. It explains the advocates' defense of the claim that the USA Tax (in contrast to rival taxes) promotes saving and investment while preserving fairness; and it details the reply of USA Tax critics. Finally, it offers recommendations for improving the design of the USA Tax.

The recommendations have one underlying theme: the USA household tax should be true to its ideal—the progressive personal consumption tax. The USA household tax should attempt to tax each household, at graduated rates, on its consumption. The central feature of the USA household tax—its unlimited savings allowance—is true to the consumption tax ideal. But in several important design details, the 1995 version of the USA Tax strays from that ideal and, in my view, gets into trouble as a consequence. Designers of the USA household tax sometimes portray it as an income tax with an unlimited savings allowance. I argue that it would be better to conceive of it and portray it as a progressive personal consumption tax, and to adhere to this concept in all the details of design.

Thus this book is fundamentally about the design of a progressive consumption tax. The USA Tax, introduced in 1995 in the U.S. Congress, comes as close as any tax bill ever considered by Congress. But whatever the fate of the USA Tax bill, this book tries to contribute to the literature on the theory and practical design of a progressive consumption tax.

Two Components

The USA Tax consists of two components: a household tax and a business tax (a concise description is given in Weidenbaum 1996). The household tax replaces the current household income tax. The business tax replaces the corporate income tax and applies to most business firms, not just corporations. The household tax will raise roughly 80% of the revenue, the business tax roughly 20%; these are the same proportions as the current income tax.

The household tax makes all household saving tax deductible. The business tax makes all business investment in capital goods (such as machinery and computers) tax deductible. These are fundamental changes from the current income tax. Why?

Under the current income tax, there are a set of limited saving deductions for retirement such as employer contributions to pension funds, individual retirement accounts, and 401(k) plans. By contrast, under the USA Tax all household saving in any amount for any purpose is tax deductible.

Under the current income tax, business investment in any capital good must be gradually deducted from revenue over the life of the good (gradually "depreciated"). By contrast, under the USA Tax, business investment in any capital good is immediately deducted from revenue (immediately "expensed").

USA Tax advocates believe that, together, these components remove two central shortcomings of the current income tax: its discouragement of households to save and its discouragement of businesses to invest. A central purpose of the USA Tax is to raise the national saving and investment rate. Its designers believe that both components promote that objective.

The Household Tax

The household USA Tax takes as its ideal the personal (household) consumption tax (sometimes called "a consumed income tax" or "expenditure tax") that has been advocated by distinguished economists over the past half century.[1] Under the personal consumption tax, each household is taxed on its consumption at graduated (progressive) rates. All saving is exempt from tax as a matter of principle. True, the USA Tax may include a few provisions that diverge from the ideal of a personal consumption tax (these are discussed primarily in chapter 4), but it is crucial to keep the ideal of a personal consumption tax foremost in mind in order to understand most of the features of the USA Tax.

The USA household tax utilizes a set of significantly graduated tax rates, introduces a new payroll tax credit, and retains the earned income tax credit. Together, these three elements preserve the degree of progressivity of the current income tax—that is, the USA Tax roughly maintains the distribution of the tax burden among high, middle, and low income classes. By contrast, the national sales tax and value-added tax have a single percentage rate. Even the flat tax, which has some graduation and progressivity because its household component has two rates—0% on the first $30,000 of wage income, and 20% for all income above this allowance[2]—significantly shifts the distribution of the tax burden from the affluent to the nonaffluent. There are four reasons for this: (1) it lacks sufficiently graduated rates; (2) it has no payroll tax credit; (3) it eliminates the earned income tax credit; and (4) it eliminates the deduction for employer contributions to health insurance. The distributional impact of the flat tax is examined in chapter 3.

If graduation were regarded as unimportant or even undesirable, there might be no need for a household tax, and its elimination would be a sweet victory for tax simplification. Some advocates of completely replacing the current income tax with a national sales tax or a VAT tantalize citizens with visions of the abolition of the Internal Revenue Service and the elimination of the need to file a return on April 15. But the majority of citizens, like USA Tax advocates, appear to favor significant graduation of rates.

Flat tax advocates accept some graduation. To achieve it, they retain the IRS and an individual tax return, but they emphasize the simplicity of their postcard-sized individual tax return. Although they describe their household tax as having a single rate, it really has two, as noted above. They correctly note that these two rates achieve some progressivity; that is, the ratio of tax to wage income rises as household wage income rises.

USA Tax proponents point out that the majority of Americans appear to believe that fairness requires a degree of progressivity roughly comparable to the current income tax—significant progressivity at the top as well as the bottom of the income (or consumption) scale—and they favor a set of tax rates that are sufficiently graduated to achieve this degree of progressivity.

For example, Sheffrin (1993) reports on a survey conducted by Hite and Roberts (1991), who asked a representative sample of taxpayers about the income tax rates they regard as fair. The mean response preferred an average tax rate (the ratio of tax to income) of 2% for the lowest income class and 27% for the highest (over $100,000 in 1991). Note that achieving an average tax rate of 27% for this class requires a top bracket rate greater than 27% (significantly higher than the 20% rate proposed by flat tax advocates). Specifically, 38% of their sample preferred rate schedules with the top bracket ("marginal") rate exceeding 45%, 28% prefer the 1991 schedule (15%, 28%, 31%), and 34% preferred a lower flat rate with an exemption.

USA Tax advocates agree that fairness requires graduated rates that achieve roughly the same distribution of the tax burden as the current income tax. Hence, although they concur that eliminating April 15 tax returns might be nice, they can't support it. In their view, genuine significant progressivity at the top as well as bottom requires a household tax with sufficiently graduated rates. Moreover, the graduated household tax must be the main revenue-raiser of the two-component (household and business) tax system.

So how does the household USA Tax differ from the household income tax? There is one fundamental difference. The USA Tax makes all saving tax deductible—it gives an unlimited savings allowance—so that it taxes each household according to its consumption, not its income. The comprehensive income tax would make no saving tax deductible, and the current income tax permits only a few limited deductions for certain kinds of retirement saving, in the process compromising the ideal of an income tax.

It is crucial to fully appreciate this fundamental difference. The ideal of the income tax is to tax all income, whether consumed or saved. Income tax reformers have sought to move the current income tax toward an ideal comprehensive income tax. Adhering to principle, they have attempted to eliminate all deductions for saving. For example, they have sought to count employer pension contributions as taxable employee income and to eliminate individual retirement account deductions. They have had both victories and defeats concerning retirement saving, but they have scored a virtually complete victory concerning saving for any other purpose.

It is often mistakenly thought that a consumption tax cannot be as progressive as an income tax. It is easy to see why this mistake occurs.

The income tax has always been a household tax with graduated rates. Traditionally, consumption taxes have been levied on business firms at a single percentage rate—the sales tax and the value-added tax. Naturally, advocates of progressivity have traditionally rallied to the income tax, and opponents of progressivity have attacked the income tax and championed the sales tax or the VAT.

But a personal consumption tax, levied on the household rather than the business firm, can use graduated rates to be every bit as progressive as the current income tax. What must be grasped is that a practical personal consumption tax is a relatively recent proposal. Consumption taxes have been levied on business firms for several thousand years. By contrast, the household income tax is roughly a century old, and the first practical blueprint for a household consumption tax is only a half century old.[3]

An advocate of significant graduation now has two choices: the graduated income tax or the graduated personal consumption tax (the household USA Tax). As always, the graduation advocate must remain wary of consumption taxes levied completely on business firms (the sales tax and the VAT) or heavily on business firms (the flat tax). But now there is a genuinely new option: the household consumption tax with significantly graduated rates. The choice between the two turns not on progressivity, but on what should be taxed: income or consumption?

To understand the personal consumption tax return, one must recognize the strategy behind it. Household consumption is financed by cash—currency or check—perhaps with a short lag after the use of a credit card. So the strategy is to follow the cash. The household must first add up cash inflows. It then subtracts nonconsumption cash outflows. What's left is consumption. This cash flow technique for computing this year's consumption is of such practical importance that the tax is sometimes called "the cash flow consumption tax."

After deducting personal exemptions and a family allowance, the household would apply the graduated tax rates to its taxable consumption to obtain its tentative tax. Finally, the household would receive a new tax credit for its share of the Social Security (FICA) payroll tax; and a household with low wage income would continue to receive the earned income tax credit. These credits would be subtracted to arrive at the household's actual tax.

It is important to emphasize that the reason for adding all cash inflows and subtracting nonconsumption cash outflows is to accurately compute this year's consumption. It is irrelevant whether a particular cash inflow is "income." What matters is whether its inclusion is necessary to correctly compute the household's consumption. Cash flow items are not taxed per se. It is computed consumption that is taxed.

Thus, on a personal consumption tax return, each household would add up cash inflows actually received, including wages and salaries, interest, and dividends, just as it does under the income tax. But unlike the income tax, it would also add cash withdrawals from savings accounts and investment funds, and receipts from the sale of stocks and bonds. In contrast to the income tax, the household would then subtract cash deposits in savings accounts and investment funds, and purchases of stocks and bonds. To compute its consumption accurately, there would be no limit to the amount it would subtract—it would have an unlimited savings allowance. Managers of each account or fund would report cash withdrawals and deposits in a calendar year to each household.

It is important to emphasize that only cash deposits and withdrawals from any account or fund are relevant to the tax return, not fluctuations in the market value of any fund's portfolio. Such fluctuations are irrelevant because the goal is to compute the household's consumption by following cash inflows and outflows. Only cash deposits and withdrawals are needed to compute the household's consumption.

The proper treatment of housing and other expensive consumer durables has been considered by designers of the personal consumption tax. Virtually all agree that it is essential to develop some practical method of spreading tax over time, rather than requiring all tax to be paid in the year of purchase. The practical options for achieving spreading are examined in chapter 4.

It might seem that the household should also be able to deduct cash outflows for taxes withheld or paid during the calendar year, because these subtractions are necessary to achieve an accurate measure of the household's private consumption. In chapter 4, I explain why the USA Tax makes all taxes (federal, state, or local) withheld or paid in the calendar year nondeductible. Thus the household's tax base is private consumption plus taxes. To the degree that taxes roughly reflect public consumption (consumption services provided to the household by government), the household's tax base roughly approximates its total consumption (private plus public).

The household tax introduces a new deduction for a limited amount of investment in human capital—expenditure on higher education and vocational training. Although businesses do most of the investment in the economy, households also perform some investment. In recognition of the economic importance of human capital, a new education deduction is included in the household tax. Higher education tuition expense up to a limit is regarded as a nonconsumption cash outflow, and is therefore deductible.

Two features of the USA Tax have nothing to do with whether the tax base is consumption or income: the new payroll tax credit and the earned income tax credit. In recent years Congress has reduced the income tax burden on low-income households, but the payroll tax for those households is still substantial. The new payroll tax credit means that the total tax (USA net tax plus employee payroll tax) on a household will equal the tax specified by the USA Tax schedule.[4] The earned income tax credit is retained, no longer to offset the Social Security payroll tax, but simply to supplement the earnings of low-wage households. Its schedule will be adjusted in light of the new payroll tax credit.

An example of a personal consumption tax return is given in table 4.1 (p. 71). Round numbers are used to simplify the example; they are not intended to embody actual USA Tax rates or amounts. All items on the return are discussed in chapter 4. It should be emphasized that the designers of the USA Tax continue to revise the practical details of the USA Tax and therefore, of the USA household tax return. This personal consumption tax return contains core elements of the USA household tax, but may differ in certain respects from the USA tax return that designers will eventually adopt. These issues are discussed in chapter 4.

Given these provisions, the designers of the USA tax have tentatively estimated the set of graduated rates and brackets that would achieve roughly the same distribution of the tax burden as the current income tax. These rates and brackets are given in the 1995 bill. For a married couple filing a joint return, the rates would initially be 0%, 19%, 27%%, and 40%; after a three-year phase-in, the rates would be 0%, 8%, 19%, and 40%. The 40% rate would begin when taxable consumption exceeds $24,000; this is much lower than the corresponding income tax threshold primarily because the USA Tax gives each household a new payroll tax credit. If the household earns and consumes another $100 of wage income, its USA net tax plus employee payroll tax together increase $40;

hence the marginal tax rate from these two taxes together is 40%, the rate specified in the USA Tax schedule. It should be emphasized that further estimation may alter the rates and brackets required to achieve the same degree of progressivity as the current income tax.

The Business Tax

The business tax is a subtraction value-added tax (VAT). It replaces the corporate income tax and applies to all business firms. Each firm would be taxed roughly 11% on the difference between its sales revenue and its purchases from other firms, including capital goods. Its most important feature is that expenditure on capital goods would be immediately deducted instead of gradually deducted (depreciated) over time as under the current income tax.

For each firm, the tax base equals value added (output) minus investment. For the business sector as a whole, therefore, the tax base is value added minus investment, which equals consumption. It is for this reason that a VAT is often called a consumption tax and that its burden is generally assumed to be borne by consumers. Thus investment is excluded from the tax base under the business tax, just as saving is excluded under the household tax. The two components of the USA Tax system therefore remove the current discouragement to business investment and household saving.

Most other countries use a credit-invoice VAT instead of a subtraction VAT. Each firm is taxed on its sales, but then given a credit for the VAT paid on its purchases. The tax computed by the subtraction method, 11% of the difference between sales and purchases, should equal the tax computed by the credit-invoice method, 11% of sales minus 11% of purchases. The practical pros and cons of each method are discussed in chapter 4. One advantage of the subtraction method in the United States is its familiarity—it is the method used under the U.S. corporate income tax. Another is that it may be easier to maintain a single rate for most firms, just as it has for the corporate income tax.

Just as the household tax gives a credit for the employee's share of the Social Security payroll tax, so the business tax gives a credit for the employer's share. The new payroll tax credit for business means that the total tax on the business firm (USA net business tax plus payroll tax) will equal the tax specified by the USA business tax schedule: roughly 11% of sales minus purchases.[5]

The business tax replaces the corporate income tax and in effect replaces the employer payroll tax (while preserving Social Security payments). It is conventionally assumed that a VAT burdens consumers, a corporate income tax burdens the owners of capital, and a payroll tax burdens workers; so the USA business component substitutes a tax on consumption for a tax on capital income and a tax on labor income. Thus the net impact on progressivity of replacing the corporate income tax with the USA business tax (with its payroll tax credit) is not obvious.

What must be emphasized is that the progressive household USA tax will raise roughly 80% of USA Tax revenue, the business USA tax only 20%. The progressivity of the household tax assures that the entire USA Tax achieves a progressive distribution of its tax burden. In particular, the household USA tax uses graduated rates, a new payroll tax credit, and the earned income credit to protect low- and moderate-income households. Thus the distributional impact of the business tax is relatively unimportant under the USA Tax.

By contrast, under a national sales tax or VAT intended to replace the household tax, the distributional impact of the business tax is crucial because it cannot be offset through a household tax. The distributional impact of the business tax is also important under the flat tax where the business tax raises perhaps half of total revenue, the household tax has a single positive rate, the earned income credit is terminated, and there is no payroll tax credit.

Besides the immediate deduction for investment, five other features of the USA business tax, a subtraction VAT, distinguish it from the current corporate income tax. First, financial transactions are ignored (except for financial institutions)—interest and dividends received are excluded, and there is no deduction for interest and dividends paid. Hence the business tax treats interest and dividends identically. This removes the current bias toward debt financing. Second, current cash flows are used to compute the firm's tax so there is no need for complex accrual accounting. Third, the tax is territorial—only goods produced in the United States will be subject to tax. This eliminates the complexity of accounting for foreign subsidiaries. Fourth, the tax is "border adjustable": export sales are excluded and imports are taxed. This enables a proper integration with the border-adjustable VATs of our trading partners. Our exports will be taxed only under the VAT of the importing country, instead of being double-taxed. Because other VATs exclude exports, imports from VAT countries will now face the same tax as our domestic producers.

Fifth, employee compensation is not deductible. This achieves a much larger tax base than the current corporate income tax, which deducts all compensation including fringe benefits and interest, and a larger base than the flat tax that deducts cash employee compensation. The larger base enables a smaller rate to raise the same revenue. Nondeductibility of compensation also reduces the number of firms with a negative tax base that entitles the firm to a tax credit that is carried forward to next year.

This Book's Outline

This chapter has given a concise description of the USA Tax. The appendix gives the interesting story of how the personal consumption tax has evolved over the past half century. Chapter 2 addresses the impact on saving; chapter 3, the issue of fairness; chapter 4, practical design options; chapter 5, simplification; and chapter 6, questions and answers.

Appendix: History of the Personal Consumption (Expenditure) Tax

The past two decades have witnessed numerous articles, conferences, and debates over the merits of converting the household income tax to a household consumption tax (also called a consumed income tax or expenditure tax). In 1992, the Strengthening of America Commission of the Center for Strategic and International Studies, co-chaired by senators Pete Domenici (R-New Mexico) and Sam Nunn (D-Georgia), endorsed conversion. The introduction of the USA Tax bill into the Senate in 1995, under the sponsorship of Domenici, Nunn, and Bob Kerrey (D-Nebraska), represents a milestone in a story that began a half century ago with the monographs of two distinguished economists: Irving Fisher of Yale University and Nicholas Kaldor of Cambridge University. In fact, as Kaldor reports, the idea of taxing personal consumption has an even older legacy.

Kaldor begins his classic monograph *An Expenditure Tax* (1955) with the following quotation from the political philosopher Thomas Hobbes (*Leviathan*, ch. 30):

...the Equality of Imposition consisteth rather in the Equality of that which is consumed, than of the riches of the persons that consume the same. For what reason is there, that he which laboureth much, and sparing the fruits of his labour, consumeth little, should be more charged, than he that living idely getteth little, and spendeth all he gets: seeing the one hath no more protection from the Commonwealth than the other? But when the Impositions are layd upon those things which men consume, every man payeth Equally for what he useth: Nor is the Common-wealth defrauded by the luxurious waste of private men.

In his introduction, Kaldor provides this interesting background to the personal consumption (expenditure) tax (pp. 11–13):

The Idea examined in this book—that the taxation of individuals should be based on their expenditure, and not on their income—is by no means a new one. The case in equity for taxing people in accordance with what they consume rather than what they earn was succinctly put 300 years ago by Hobbes. It was re-stated, on rather different grounds, just over one hundred years ago in the *Principles of Political Economy* by John Stuart Mill who argued the case at length on several occasions, particularly before the Select Committee on Income and Property Tax in 1861. Mill's advocacy was taken up by a row of distinguished economists like Marshall and Pigou in England, Irving Fisher in the United States and Luigi Einaudi in Italy. There can be few ideas in the field of economics which are so revolutionary in their implications and yet can look back on so respectable an ancestry...

Kaldor notes that the main stumbling block was thought to be practicality:

Full exploration of the problem was delayed also by the persistent conviction that studying the merits of such a tax was largely an academic exercise—for it was taken for granted that the administrative difficulties involved in assessing people on their spending were too great for this "ideal" system of taxation to be put into practice. Thus Mill himself, having declared before the Select Committee that the only "perfectly unexceptionable and just principle of income tax" is to "exempt all savings", went on to say that the "amount of saving cannot be got at in an individual case" and all that a tax system could do in deference to the principle is to tax those incomes more leniently which can be presumed to give rise to more savings, since they are temporary in duration and precarious in character. Similarly, Marshall, in suggesting that a graduated tax on personal expenditure is superior to all other forms of taxation, direct or indirect, described the tax as a "Utopian goal", though he added that "the way to this ideal perfection is difficult but it is more clearly marked than in regard to most Utopian goals". Professor Pigou, both in his book on Public Finance, and his evidence before the Colwyn Committee on National Debt and Taxation, referred to the impossibility of preventing dishonest citizens making a practice of "saving in one year, thus escaping taxation, and secretly selling out and spending their savings in the next year". Keynes, in his own evidence before the Colwyn Committee, dismissed the Expenditure Tax in a sentence by saying that while the tax is "perhaps theoretically sound, it is practically impossible".

Kaldor explains that the great breakthrough on practicality came from Irving Fisher of Yale in 1937:

This indeed summed up the attitude of most economists. It was not until Irving Fisher relatively late in life, and after a lifetime spent in applying the principles of double entry book-keeping to a theoretical analysis of Capital and Income, discovered that the net savings or dis-savings of individuals can be computed on much the same accounting principles as business savings are computed, that the question assumed a new significance. Fisher's original paper, published early in 1937, attracted little notice. His subsequent writings in various periodicals, and his book on the subject published during the war, must have been instrumental, however, in getting the United States Treasury interested to the point of putting before Congress in September 1942 a proposal for a progressive spendings tax as their principal suggestion for war finance. In this country, possibly owing to the interruption in the international flow of ideas caused by the war, Fisher's work attracted no notice whatever, and as far as I know, his book has never been reviewed in any of the English periodicals.

Let us quote the beginning of the path-breaking book, *Constructive Income Taxation*, by Irving Fisher and his brother Herbert Fisher, who write (1942, pp. 3–6):

Although this book aims primarily to show ways in which income taxation can be improved in wartime—even if only a little—we shall begin by showing what we believe to be the ideal and permanent solution of the whole problem, valid in both peace and war. We fully realize that it is too much to expect such an ideal program to be fully adopted at once. But, by setting the ideal clearly before us as an ultimate goal, we may guide our steps toward it more surely.

An entirely new approach to income tax legislation has long been needed.... In our opinion, the present income taxes are objectionable in many ways. For instance:

(1) They are unfair, both to the taxpayer and to the government, not only because they impose double taxation (by taxing savings and their fruits) ... but also because they thus tax the producers of the nation's wealth more heavily than those who merely spend, especially the "idle rich."

(2) By taxing the increase in capital, they kill the most important geese which lay the most important golden eggs.

(3) They are unwise, largely because they actually kill much of the revenue which they should produce...

THE TAX BASE

The essential feature of our proposal is that the proposed tax base is *income spent,* that is, income used for consumption purposes, excluding all *income saved*, such as undivided profits and investments, presumably used for productive purposes.

As the Fishers readily admit, their proposal is not new. They modestly write that the only contribution they have to make concerns practicality. They write:

> Essentially the same proposal—to tax only so much of the gross income as is spent, not saved—has been praised as "ideal" by John Stuart Mill, Professor Alfred Marshall, Professor Arthur C. Pigou, Professor Luigi Einaudi, and others; but most of these authorities have regarded this ideal as unattainable because (so they thought) "spendings" can be measured only by means of records which might be incomplete and incorrect.
>
> It is strange that those who recognize that "spendings" are the only fair and logical base for taxable income often fail to realize how practical and simple is its application.
>
> How do we figure what we spend in a day? We need only two data:
>
> 1. The amount we had to spend; that is, what we had or received during the day.
>
> 2. The amount we did not spend; that is, the amount left over as determined by counting at the end of the day.
>
> The application of this simple procedure to the tax problem is the only novelty in the present proposal.
>
> Moreover, the data needed for this calculation are considerably more trustworthy than those used in our present income taxes, which often depend on debatable estimates.
>
> We propose, then, to reckon taxable spendings, not by adding together the separate items spent for food, clothing, rent, amusements, etc., but by adding together the *gross receipts from all sources* and then deducting all items of outgo *other* than "spendings." The chief deductions under this proposal are: investments, taxes paid during the taxable year, and proper exemptions for the taxpayer and his dependents.

They then emphasize the advantage of their household consumption tax over a sales tax by starting their explanation with this section heading:

THE TAX WOULD BE A LUXURY TAX

> It will be seen that our proposed new income tax is not merely a spendings tax; it is practically a *luxury*-spendings tax—"luxury" being defined as any excess above reasonable necessities. These necessities would mostly escape the tax through the "minimum exemptions." Thus, unlike a sales tax, this luxury tax would allow little or no taxing of necessities; and would spare the spendings of the very poor. The middle class and the rich would bear the burden; for, the greater the spendings—which means the more luxurious—the higher the rate.

Such a luxury-spendings tax is more truly a luxury tax than any excise tax on specific luxuries, such as costly automobiles, opera tickets, or Oriental rugs. To define satisfactorily specific objects as "luxuries" is impossible; but to *measure* satisfactorily what constitutes luxurious *spending,* and with definite gradations, is easy.

They also introduce the term "net cash yield tax" that captures the practical method of computation. Today a similar term, "cash flow tax," conveys the same point. They write:

WOULD ALSO BE A NET CASH YIELD TAX

To this proposed tax, either of two names may be applied—one, as just indicated, in terms of disbursements and the other in terms of receipts:

(1) it is a tax on spendings;
(2) it is a tax on what is here called net cash yield.

Net cash yield may be defined as the gross payments received by the taxpayer in the taxable year *from* all income sources, less any payments he may make *into* income sources *during that same year,* and less certain other deductions to be specified by law.

Kaldor's 1955 monograph kept the proposal alive and advanced the case for its adoption (some important passages from his book will be quoted in chapter 3). But it wasn't until the mid-1970s that a new surge of interest and analysis took place in the United States, Britain, and several European countries. Under the leadership of economist David Bradford, on leave from Princeton, the U.S. Treasury produced *Blueprints for Basic Tax Reform* (1977), which examined in great practical detail both a comprehensive income tax and a cash flow consumption tax. In its introduction (2d ed., 1984, pp. 2–3), the report states:

This study shows that it is feasible to have a broadly based tax that departs in major ways from the current tax law. In providing specific alternative plans, the report sets out a guide for future legislation aimed at sweeping tax reform. It also points out some of the major policy issues that remain to be resolved. In presenting a plan for a tax system based on the consumption concept, the report points toward a promising alternative approach to tax reform that is not as different from our present system as it might seem and that, if consistently implemented, should provide major advantages in fairness, simplicity, and economic efficiency.

In Britain, under the leadership of economics Nobel laureate James Meade of Cambridge, a lengthy and detailed report was issued by the Institute for Fiscal Studies entitled *The Structure and Reform of Direct Taxation* (1978). The report concludes (p. 502):

A progressive expenditure tax gives the maximum opportunity for business enterprise and development (since all resources devoted to such development are free of tax); but at the same time it imposes a heavy tax on heavy spending by the wealthy, including expenditure out of capital resources.... For these reasons, all of us with the exception of one member of the Committee have a decided preference for moves in the direction of an expenditure tax, provided that the problems of transition can be met.

2   Saving

Why convert the income tax to the unlimited savings allowance (USA) Tax? According to most USA Tax advocates, a central reason is to raise the saving rate of the U.S. economy. But is this important? And will the USA Tax actually raise the saving rate?

Dismal Fact: The United States Is a Low-Saving Country

Most Americans appear unaware of two economic facts that are crucial to our future relative and absolute standard of living. First, the United States has maintained a lower saving rate than most other economically advanced countries for several decades. Second, the U.S. saving rate has declined over the past two decades. Tables 2.1 and 2.2 tell the story.

Table 2.1 shows gross saving as a percentage of gross domestic product (GDP) for the Organization for Economic Cooperation and Development (OECD) countries for the 1960s, 1970s, and 1980s, and from 1990 to 1992. The table lists the countries in the order of their 1980s ranking. Gross saving includes the gross saving of households, firms, and government. Of the twenty-three OECD countries, the United States ranked nineteenth in the 1960s, twenty-first in the 1970s, eighteenth in the 1980s, and twenty-first in the first three years of the 1990s. While the leaders of the 1980s, Japan and Switzerland, saved 31.7% and 28.5% respectively, the United States managed to save only 17.7%.

Table 2.2 shows net saving as a percentage of net national income for the five OECD countries with the largest GDPs in 1992. Net saving equals gross saving minus the depreciation of the capital stock; hence net saving indicates the saving in excess of what is required merely to

Table 2.1
Gross saving as a percentage of GDP

	1960s		1970s		1980s		1990–1992	
	Rank	%	Rank	%	Rank	%	Rank	%
Japan	1	34.5	1	35.3	1	31.7	1	34.3
Switzerland	2	29.4	2	28.6	2	28.5	2	30.2
Norway	6	27.4	4	26.8	3	27.7	7	23.5
Austria	4	27.7	3	28.0	4	24.3	4	25.8
Portugal	15	23.1	6	26.0	5	24.3	3	25.9
Finland	9	25.4	5	26.7	6	24.2	17	17.3
Netherlands	5	27.6	11	24.9	7	23.1	6	24.9
Germany	7	27.3	13	24.3	8	22.3	8	23.5
Italy	3	28.1	7	25.9	9	22.0	13	18.7
Spain	11	24.7	10	25.5	10	21.1	10	20.9
Canada	17	21.9	16	22.9	11	20.7	19	15.4
Australia	12	24.7	14	24.1	12	20.6	16	17.9
France	8	26.2	8	25.8	13	20.5	11	20.7
New Zealand	18	21.2	17	22.2	14	20.1	15	18.1
Turkey	23	14.8	23	17.1	15	19.3	12	19.8
Iceland	10	25.4	12	24.8	16	18.7	20	15.4
Ireland	21	18.4	18	21.3	17	18.4	5	25.0
United States	**19**	**19.9**	**21**	**19.6**	**18**	**17.7**	**21**	**15.1**
Greece	20	19.2	9	25.8	19	17.7	22	14.9
Sweden	13	24.0	19	21.1	20	17.7	18	16.5
Belgium	16	22.4	15	23.1	21	16.9	9	21.3
United Kingdom	22	18.4	22	17.9	22	16.6	23	13.8
Denmark	14	23.3	20	20.9	23	15.4	14	18.6

Source: OECD National Accounts, presented in OECD 1994b, table 2.1, pp. 21–24.

offset depreciation. Positive net saving is necessary to actually increase the capital stock. Net national income equals gross national income minus depreciation.

Of the five largest (by GDP) OECD countries, the United States had the smallest net saving rate in all three decades by a wide margin, well below the average of all OECD countries. The net saving rate of all five countries (and the whole OECD) declined from the 1970s to the 1980s; however, in the early 1990s, Japan and Germany halted their decline—Japan at 23.0%, Germany at 12.4%—while the U.S. net saving rate declined to just 2.5%.

Table 2.2
Net saving as a percentage of net national income

	1970s	1980s	1990–1992
Japan	25.6	20.9	23.0
Germany	15.1	11.2	12.4
France	17.1	9.0	8.7
Italy	16.4	11.2	7.6
United States	**9.1**	**5.2**	**2.5**
OECD	13.8	9.7	8.7

Source: OECD 1994a; percentages computed by the author.

Is Saving Important?

What's so important about saving? Saving is the key to the future standard of living (Seidman 1990b, chapter 2). Saving finances investment in plant, equipment, technology, research, development, education, and training. In turn, this accumulation of capital raises output per worker—"productivity." Finally, higher output per worker makes possible higher consumption per worker—a higher standard of living.

Let's ask a basic question. What causes a nation to gradually raise its standard of living over several decades? Although many factors contribute, one deserves center stage: the accumulation of capital. Capital is anything that lifts a worker's productivity—the output (goods or services) that a worker can produce in a given period of time.

One kind of capital is physical capital. Give a farmer a tractor, a factory worker equipment, or an office worker a computer, and productivity rises. Build a bridge, a highway, or a telecommunications network, and productivity rises. Glance back two centuries and observe the American worker struggling to produce with primitive tools, or look abroad today to poor countries where workers engage in the same struggle, and you will grasp the power of physical capital to raise worker productivity.

But capital includes more than physical capital. It is also knowledge capital, the stock of technical knowledge accumulated from past experience and research. A stock of blueprints prescribes how to make particular goods and services. Imagine what would happen if we suddenly lost those blueprints. We would have to reinvent the wheel and everything else. So knowledge is also a vital component of capital.

Finally, capital includes human capital, the skill of the workforce that results from education and training. The stock of blueprints and machinery won't do much good if workers aren't educated and trained to follow the blueprints and operate the machines.

Now that the power of capital is apparent, how do we get more of it? How do we accumulate capital? Every year we must undertake investment that exceeds the depreciation (wearing out) of old capital. Suppose the capital stock is $10 trillion on January 1, and during the year $1 trillion wears out from use. If this year we produce $2 trillion of new capital, then next January 1 our capital stock will be $11 trillion.

So how do we produce enough investment goods? Investment must be financed by saving. Firms can finance the purchase of investment goods only by tapping saving—their own retained earnings or the saving of households. If households save more, they make more funds available to banks that lend to business firms, or they buy more corporate stocks and bonds or they put more saving into managed funds that do the same thing, again enabling firms to finance more investment.

A higher saving rate sounds nice, but by definition it implies a lower consumption rate. Saving is defined as income that is not consumed. If we raise our national "saving rate" (the ratio of saving to income) from 20% to 24%, we are by definition reducing our "consumption rate" (the ratio of consumption to income) from 80% to 76%.

So there is another way to see what is required to produce more investment goods—a way that illuminates the short-run sacrifice. Our workforce is divided between making consumer goods and investment goods. With a fully employed workforce, if more workers make investment goods, less are available to make consumer goods. If we raise the share of our workforce making investment goods from 20% to 24%, then the share making consumer goods must fall from 80% to 76%. So we face a trade-off. The higher our investment rate (percentage) today, the greater will be our capital stock, output, and consumption tomorrow. But the lower must be our consumption rate (percentage) today.

Does this mean we must cut this year's consumption below last year's? Must we have a recession? No. But we must be careful. We must phase in the increase in our investment rate very gradually. Here's how. Normally, real (inflation-adjusted) output in the U.S. economy grows about 2.5% per year; so do consumption and investment. What we seek is to make investment goods grow faster than 2.5% for a few years, and accept growth in consumption goods that is positive but less than 2.5% for a few years. During this transition, consumption would grow more slowly than usual, the investment rate would rise gradually, and the consumption rate would decline gradually. Job growth would be faster in the investment goods sector and slower in the consumer goods sector. When workers retire or quit in the consumer goods sector, they would often not be replaced. But gradualism can avoid layoffs. Once the transition is complete, both sectors can once again grow at the same rate—a rate that will be a bit higher than today due to the permanently higher investment rate and the faster accumulation of capital.

Before long, output and consumption will be permanently higher than they otherwise would have been due to our temporary sacrifice. But how much higher? And how long will the sacrifice take; that is, what is "the sacrifice time"—the time during which consumption, though still growing, is below the level it otherwise would have attained?

My colleague Ken Lewis and I try to answer these questions for the U.S. economy (Lewis and Seidman 1994) by fitting a translog production function to the data of the U.S. economy for the most recent four decades. The two factors of production are labor input and a vintage capital stock that we constructed. The vintage capital stock recognizes the fact that more recent capital is more productive because it embodies technical progress. Then we simulate an increase in the U.S. investment rate, focusing on the private gross investment rate, which initially is about 15% (the total investment rate including government purchase investment is closer to 20%). We consider a phased increase to 18% (a 20% increase over the initial 15%) over either three or six years to allow time for the economy to absorb the shift in the composition of output without a significant recession.

Here's what we find. Although capital and output per worker rises immediately, consumption per worker initially grows more slowly than it otherwise would. If the increase in the investment rate were abrupt, the sacrifice time would be only half a decade, but with a more prudent phase-in, the sacrifice time is just under a decade. Thus in less than a decade, the sacrifice is over as consumption per worker attains the level it would have had if the investment rate had never increased. From then on consumption per worker is permanently higher than it otherwise would have been. After five decades, output per worker is 10% higher each year, and consumption per worker—the standard of living—6% higher each year than it would have been without the increase in the investment rate. How great are the long-run gains compared to the short-run losses? The "investment rate return"—the discount rate that makes the present value of the long-run gains equal the present value of the short-run losses—is roughly 13%, surely a respectable rate of return.

But how can firms making investment goods be induced to grow faster than normal during the transition? They will do it if other firms place orders at a faster rate. It is the job of the Federal Reserve to induce firms to place more orders. If the Fed brings down interest rates, then firms will find it profitable to borrow more to buy more investment goods. So the Fed is the key to faster growth in the investment goods sector.

How can firms making consumer goods be induced to grow slower than normal for a few years? They will do it if households slow their growth in consumption demand. And what will make households do this? Something must make households gradually increase their saving rate (the percentage of their income they save), thereby gradually reducing their consumption rate (the percentage of their income they consume). Exhortation won't do it. But a fundamental change in tax policy has a good chance to succeed. Conversion of the income tax to any consumption tax (sales tax, VAT, flat tax, or USA Tax) would give households an incentive to raise their saving rate. I'll examine the effectiveness of tax conversion in a moment.

Another Dismal Fact: Slow U.S. Productivity Growth

Now that we see there is a short-run sacrifice, it is natural to hope that our current growth in productivity (output per hour worked) is fast enough so we don't have to raise our saving rate. Unfortunately, that is not the case. Here's what economists on the Council of Economic Advisors reported in the *Economic Report of the President* (1992, pp. 92–93):

Growth in capital per worker is, over long periods of time, closely associated with productivity growth. From 1959 to 1973, for example, capital per worker grew by 2.4 percent a year in the private business sector, while productivity in that sector grew by 2.8 percent. From 1973 to 1989, capital per worker grew at 0.8 percent annually and annual productivity growth was 0.9 percent...

Studies ... find a high correlation between investment rates and rates of productivity growth in different countries. Among major industrialized countries, the United States had the lowest investment rate and the lowest rate of productivity growth in recent decades. According to a recent OECD survey, U.S. gross investment as a fraction of gross national product averaged 19 percent in 1971-80, and 18 percent in 1981–89; the corresponding figure for Japan was 29 percent. Between 1950 and 1979, the United States had the lowest rate of growth of capital per worker among the "group of seven" industrial countries (the others being Canada, France, Germany, Italy, Japan, and the United Kingdom).

Have things improved since then? According to the most recent *Economic Report of the President* (Council of Economic Advisors 1996, p. 58), very little. These are the latest measures of U.S. productivity growth: output per hour in nonfarm business grew at an annual rate of 2.9% from 1960 to 1973, 1.1% from 1973 to 1981, and 1.1% from 1981 to 1995; the *Report* forecasts a growth rate of 1.2% from 1995 to 2002.

Investment and the Real Wage of Workers

Not surprisingly, real (inflation-adjusted) wage growth has declined with productivity growth. Slow wage growth would be bad enough if workers of all skill levels—high and low—crept forward at the same slow rate. But as we will see in chapter 3, recently an ominous inequality has been superimposed on slow average growth: low-skilled wages have grown much more slowly than high-skilled wages and in many instances have actually fallen.

Taking the long view, capital accumulation has been the key to raising the real wages of workers of all skill levels over many decades. Certain machinery has boosted the productivity primarily of high-skilled workers, while other machinery has lifted the productivity of low-skilled workers. Whether capital accumulation has generally boosted one at a faster rate than the other is an interesting question. But in absolute terms, it has raised the real wage of both. Over the long run, capital accumulation has been an effective antipoverty "program" for the vast majority of low-skilled persons able and willing to work.

Citizens concerned about the recent failure of many low-skilled workers to improve their wages should make a higher investment rate a top priority. In the short run, low-wage workers can be helped by the earned income tax credit that takes the low-wage as given and provides a government supplement. But in the long run, low-wage workers need faster capital accumulation, generated by a higher national investment rate, to raise their productivity and wage.

How much difference can a higher investment rate make? In a recent empirical study, Ken Lewis and I try to answer this question for the U.S. economy (Lewis and Seidman 1993). We divide the U.S. labor force

into low- and high-educated labor, and fit a translog production function to U.S. data for a recent twenty-year period. We then simulate the
impact of a phased increase in the U.S. investment rate on the marginal
productivity (the addition to output that results from an additional unit
of labor) of both kinds of labor. According to economic theory, the real
wage tends to equal the marginal productivity of labor, so a worker's
pay tends to rise when her or his productivity rises.

Here's what we find. If we phase in a 20% increase in the U.S.
investment rate (for example, if the private gross investment rate
increases from 15% to 18%—by 20% of itself) over a three-year period,
in a decade the real wage of low-educated labor would be 3% higher
than it otherwise would have been, and 4% higher in two decades.
High-educated labor would do even better; its wage would be 5% higher in a decade, and 9% higher in two decades.

Thus we estimate that a phased increase in the U.S. investment rate
would raise the absolute real wage of low-skilled workers. At the same
time, their wage would not rise as much as that of high-skilled workers.
What policy conclusion should be drawn? If we give top priority to the
absolute wage and standard of living of low-skilled workers, then a
higher investment rate will deliver it. If we are also concerned about the
increase in inequality that might result, we can offset it by raising the
progressivity of the tax system.

This raises a key point. Conversion to any consumption tax—retail
sales, value-added, flat tax, or USA Tax—is likely to result in a lower
national consumption rate, and with proper policy by the Federal
Reserve, a higher national investment rate. Hence any consumption tax
is likely to raise the real wage of all workers, including low-skilled
workers. But only the USA Tax, with its graduated household tax rates,
can potentially counter any increase in inequality between low- and
high-wage workers that might occur. USA Tax rates can be made somewhat more graduated should greater inequality in earnings in fact
emerge. This option is not available with the other consumption taxes.

A Traditional Economic Argument for Raising the Saving Rate

Although non-economists often find the preceding arguments persuasive, some professional economists respond more cautiously. They reason that if the market results in a particular national saving rate, that
rate, however low, may be optimal. Average Japanese citizens may pre-

fer future to present consumption, just as they prefer rice to potatoes. But if economists respect citizens' preferences, then they should no more interfere with the citizens' choices between future and present consumption than that between rice and potatoes. U.S. economists oppose using the tax system to induce Americans to switch from potatoes to rice, so why should they support using it to induce Americans to switch from present to future consumption?

Thus, for some economists, the burden of proof is on those who doubt the optimality of the current national saving rate, however low it may be relative to other economically advanced nations. Fair enough. Let's see whether the case for using the tax system to raise saving can meet this tougher standard. I will present a traditional argument and a novel argument (Seidman 1989).

Most economists would be incensed if anyone questioned allowing the free market to decide the quantities of rice versus potatoes. These economists would be the first to agree, however, that if we taxed rice but not potatoes, the market allocation would be distorted and undesirable ("inefficient"); it would generate too little rice relative to potatoes.

But the U.S. economy indirectly taxes future consumption by taxing capital income as a component of the current income tax. Capital income taxes reduce the future consumption that can be obtained from a given amount of saving. The choice between future and present consumption is therefore currently distorted, and the saving rate that emerges from the distorted market is suspect, not sacred. It is likely that without the distortion of taxes on future consumption, the saving rate would be higher.

Another source of distortion is the U.S. Social Security system. Social Security has made a great contribution to the well-being of the elderly for many decades. But many people surely save less, knowing that Social Security will help out when they retire. Social Security offsets only a fraction of this fall in private saving with its own Trust Fund saving (surplus). In fact, until the 1983 Social Security financing reform, Social Security didn't save at all: annual benefits paid out to retirees were roughly equal to annual payroll tax revenues. Thus it is likely that the national saving rate with Social Security has been less than what the market would have generated without Social Security.

The same argument applies to two other government insurance programs: unemployment insurance and Medicare. Without these government insurance policies, it is likely that many citizens would save more to prepare for the possibility of being laid off or needing medical care in old age. Thus government social insurance, although generating great benefits for the citizenry, has almost surely reduced the national saving rate.

A final source of distortion is government saving, an important component of national saving. Government saving is not market-generated, but is determined politically by Congress and the president. The political process may generate less government saving than citizens would prefer if they understood its future implications. Politicians may believe it is easier for voters to appreciate a tax cut or benefit increase than to grasp the future gain that will result from government saving.

Thus the traditional economic argument can be summarized this way. The current national saving rate has been distorted by government interventions—capital income taxes, social insurance programs (Social Security, unemployment insurance, and Medicare), and political incentives for government dissaving. As a result, it is likely that the current saving rate is well below what it would be without these interventions. This does not mean that all the interventions were a mistake. Great benefits have come from government social insurance programs. But it does mean that the current U.S. saving rate is below the social optimum and ought to be raised by appropriate policies.

A Novel Economic Argument for Raising the Saving Rate

This novel argument is based on the concept of a public good as defined in public finance economics. Any public finance economics text teaches that certain goods are non-exclusionary: even if someone refuses to pay for the good, we cannot prevent that person from benefiting from it. We can exclude you from enjoying a television if you refuse to pay for it, so a television is a private good. But if we improve the police protection in your area, we cannot exclude you from benefiting even if you refuse to pay, so police protection is a public good.

"The market" will generate too little of a public good because of the free-rider problem. Selfish citizens will not voluntarily pay for the good if they can benefit without financing it. And if others refuse to finance the good, selfish citizens think that their contribution will be insignificant. Though not all citizens are selfish, a public good will generally be undersupplied by the market.

The textbook solution is compulsory taxation. Don't expect the market to supply adequate police protection because selfish citizens will

free-ride and refuse to pay. True, some public-spirited citizens will contribute anyway, but why should the public-spirited be made to subsidize the selfish? So compulsion is desirable to provide the optimal
provision of the public good. Acting on their own through the market,
individuals will get too little of the public good. These citizens, para-
doxically, would all judge that they were better off if they were subject
to appropriate compulsory taxation.

It can be argued that at least three public goods are relevant to the
optimality of the U.S. saving rate: (1) the international ranking of the
future U.S. standard of living, (2) poverty reduction for low-skilled people willing to work, and (3) our contribution to the "ascent of man"
through technological progress. Let me explain what each is, why each
is a public good, and how this fact affects the optimality of our saving
rate.

Today, the U.S. standard of living still ranks first internationally, but
within a few decades our relatively low saving rate will probably lower
this ranking. If the typical American wants her grandchildren to live in a
nation with a first-ranked standard of living, with the psychological,
political, and military corollaries of that fact, what can she do? She can
of course save privately to provide for her own heirs. But she cannot
influence the nation's future standard-of-living ranking through her
own saving. That future ranking is a public good for all Americans,
because any selfish citizen can reason, "If others save and I don't, our
future ranking will remain first, and I will enjoy that fact as much as any
saver. On the other hand, if I save and others don't, my sacrifice hardly
affects the future ranking."

Many citizens and politicians appear to have considerable interest in
whether Japan or Germany will overtake us economically, and whether
our grandchildren will enjoy the most advanced economy on the globe.
This implies that the international ranking of the future U.S. standard of
living is a public good that many citizens value. Yet the market will
undersupply it. It is therefore possible that many citizens would judge
that they were better off if they were all induced, perhaps even com-
pelled, to save more.

Now consider poverty reduction. As I explained earlier, most economists agree that raising the saving rate will make capital per worker
rise faster, and this will make the productivity and the real wage of
low-skilled workers grow faster. Hence raising the saving rate will
reduce absolute poverty faster for low-skilled people willing to work.

Many citizens seem to value faster poverty reduction for such people. Yet such poverty reduction is a public good. Any selfish citizen can reason, "If others save more so that poverty declines faster, I will enjoy witnessing the reduction almost as much as any saver." So each waits for others to save for this noble purpose.

Finally, consider the ascent of man. Many citizens appear to feel a pride in the quest of mankind to improve its lot and surmount new challenges. Technological progress has been a key ingredient in this historical drama. For millennia, humans have devised new products and new processes. Inventions, innovations, and breakthroughs have lifted mankind in each era. Obviously, there are dangers as well as great benefits, dislocations as well as advances. But most citizens appear willing to keep technological progress driving forward while at the same time trying to safeguard against potential hazards.

It is likely that raising the saving rate will speed the rate of technical advance and hopefully the ascent of man. Surely many citizens want their own generation to contribute to the ascent through further technological progress. Yet such a contribution is a public good. A selfish citizen can think, "If others save more, then technical progress will be faster and I will enjoy watching mankind's progress almost as much as any saver."

Let me summarize. A traditional economic argument for raising the saving rate contends that the current saving rate is less than the market would generate if there were no government interventions like capital income taxes, government social insurance programs, and political incentives for government dissaving. A novel economic argument for raising the saving rate is that there are at least three public goods—the international ranking of the future U.S. standard of living, poverty reduction, and the ascent of man—that are undersupplied by the market, and that more saving is required to supply the optimal quantities of these public goods. Together, both economic arguments provide a rationale for policies aimed at raising the U.S. saving rate that many (though not all) economists should find persuasive.

Will the USA Tax Raise the Saving Rate?

Will the USA Tax actually raise the saving rate? There are three distinct ways that the USA Tax is likely to raise national saving: the incentive effect, the horizontal redistribution (heterogeneity) effect, and the postponement effect (Seidman 1980, 1987, chapters 10 and 16; 1990b, chapter 3). Let's discuss each in turn.

The incentive effect seems obvious to non-economists: "The USA Tax gives me a tax deduction for saving, so I have a financial incentive to save more." But not all economists agree that the incentive will actually raise an individual's saving. Why not? Some economists argue that households should respond to a saving deduction the same way they respond to a rise in the interest rate because each raises the payoff or return to saving. A saving deduction gets you out of tax when you save. Do the arithmetic and you'll find you get a higher payoff from $100 of saving. Similarly, a rise in the interest rate means you get a higher payoff from putting $100 in the bank.

Economists have analyzed the effect of a rise in the interest rate and they point out that in theory the impact on saving could go either way. Why? True, you might be inclined to save more due to the greater future payoff of each dollar saved. Economists call this "the substitution effect." But on the other hand, the higher interest rate has made you richer, just like a higher wage; why not consume a little more now—save a little less—and still consume a little more in retirement? Economists call this "the income effect."

However, the replacement of the income tax by a personal consumption tax does not make households richer. The average household—whether high, middle, or low income—pays the same tax as before. So there is no income effect for the average household, just a substitution effect encouraging more saving (Seidman 1987, pp. 674–677). Economists are right about the ambiguous effect of a higher interest rate on saving due to the clash of the substitution effect and the income effect. But it is crucial to recognize that conversion to a personal consumption tax entails only the substitution effect, not the income effect, so it should induce the typical person to save more.

Now let's consider the horizontal redistribution, or heterogeneity, effect (Seidman 1980, 1984b, 1987, pp. 671–674, 1990b, pp. 44–46; Seidman and Maurer 1982, 1984; Summers 1984a; Lewis and Seidman 1996). Imagine two persons, Saver (S) and Consumer (C), who each earn exactly $1 million. Conveniently, they are extremists. After taxes, S saves everything while C consumes everything. Under a 20% income tax, each pays $200,000 in tax, so total revenue is $400,000; S saves $800,000 while C consumes $800,000, so total saving is $800,000 (all from S) while total consumption is $800,000 (all from C).

Now suppose the income tax is converted to a personal consumption tax. To be equally progressive, the consumption tax must again extract $400,000 of revenue from the two millionaires. Because S will owe no tax under the consumption tax, all $400,000 in revenue must come from C, so a 40% tax rate will do the trick. With no tax, S will save $1,000,000. C will consume $600,000. Hence total saving will rise to $1,000,000 (all from S) while total consumption will fall to $600,000 (all from C).

What has happened? Conversion to the consumption tax has shifted $200,000 of disposable (after-tax) income from C to S. The shift is horizontal because both are millionaires. C would have consumed the $200,000; S saves all $200,000. As a result, total saving rises $200,000 and total consumption falls $200,000. Thus conversion to the consumption tax shifts cash out of the hands of the affluent consumer and into the hands of the affluent saver. Of course, when people are less extreme about saving and consuming, the increase in total saving is smaller, but there is still a horizontal shifting of disposable income and a resulting increase in aggregate saving.

In two recent empirical studies, Ken Lewis and I investigate the heterogeneity (horizontal redistribution) effect using actual U.S. data (Lewis and Seidman 1996a and 1996b). We estimate that the increase in aggregate saving due solely to the heterogeneity effect of tax conversion might be roughly 11%.

The horizontal redistribution effect has been overlooked by virtually all researchers who study the impact of tax policy on saving. These researchers focus on how the representative individual responds to a change in the after-tax return to saving. An exception is Summers (1984a, p. 250), who writes:

Consider a population made up of "rule of thumb savers," each of whom saves a fixed fraction of his or her total disposable income regardless of the rate of return. The rule of thumb rate of saving varies across individuals; some are liquidity constrained and consume everything, others may have a quite high marginal propensity to save. Now imagine a reduction in the tax rate on capital income, financed by an equal revenue yield increase in the labor income tax rate. Such a measure would, assuming some persistence in savings propensities, redistribute income from persons with low- to persons with high-savings propensities. As a consequence national savings would increase, even though no individual's savings incentive was affected. As time passes, the savings rate will rise further, as the share of total income going to persons with high-savings propensities increases.

Finally, consider the postponement effect (Summers 1981; Seidman 1983, 1984a, 1990b, pp. 48–49; Auerbach and Kotlikoff 1987). Imagine that the typical person plans sensibly for retirement. He saves as a worker so he can dissave as a retiree. Conversion to a personal consumption tax will cut his tax as a worker and raise his tax as a retiree. Hence, relative to the income tax, the consumption tax postpones some of a person's tax to later in life, so the typical worker will save more and achieve a higher peak wealth at the beginning of retirement (and the typical retiree will dissave more). Because every dollar of saving generates a dollar of investment, and every dollar of wealth, a dollar of capital, the consumption tax economy will accumulate more capital per worker than the income tax economy. Moreover, in an economy with growing population and growing real wages, the greater saving of workers will outweigh the greater dissaving of retirees, so that aggregate net saving will increase. Hence the consumption tax economy will have a higher saving rate than the income tax economy because tax is postponed for the typical person.

Is there an ironclad guarantee that the incentive, horizontal redistribution, and postponement effects will together cause a significant increase in the saving rate? Alas, no guarantee is possible. Even if other countries had tried such a conversion, its impact might be hard to interpret. If saving rose, maybe something else caused it. If saving fell, maybe it would have fallen further without tax conversion. A sound study must control for other forces influencing the saving rate. But this isn't easy. The fact is, however, that other countries have not yet tried a conversion to the personal consumption tax. So we don't even have an experience to try to interpret. No one can be sure whether it will work.

Economists have done quite a few studies trying to estimate the impact of limited, restricted saving incentives such as the individual retirement account (IRA). Although some studies find no impact on saving (Engen, Gale, and Scholz 1994), others detect a significant impact (Venti and Wise 1990). Researchers who find no impact suggest that people simply shift the $2,000 they would otherwise save in a bank to an IRA (recall that the IRA ceiling has been $2,000). Researchers who detect an impact counter that people shift some, but not all, of such saving into an IRA. For example, instead of putting $2,000 in the bank, perhaps they put $1,000 in the bank, place the other $1,000 into the IRA, and increase saving by still another $1,000 to reach the IRA ceiling of

$2,000, thereby raising their total saving from $2,000 to $3,000 in response to the IRA.

What deserves emphasis is that the unlimited savings allowance differs from the limited, restricted savings allowances that have been studied. If a person weighs contributing to an IRA, he must worry about whether he will need the cash before retirement. Even if he is willing to take his chance, the amount that is tax deductible is limited. The USA Tax removes the worry. Save today if you can get by today. If something comes up tomorrow, you can withdraw your funds without any special penalty or restriction. Save as much as you can today; there is no limit to how much is tax deductible. Thus these studies cannot tell us what would happen to saving under the USA Tax. No recent experience can.

Some analysts (Steurle 1996; Bernheim 1996) suggest that conversion to a personal consumption tax may reduce employer contributions to pension funds because all saving, not just retirement saving, will be tax deductible. They wonder whether households will have the self-discipline to save as much as employers saved on their behalf through the current pension system. They predict that in an effort to attract funds, pensions will remove restrictions and penalties on preretirement withdrawals. They wonder whether households will have the self-discipline to resist tapping their savings accounts and investment funds to finance preretirement consumption.

It is possible, however, that pension fund saving may actually increase under a personal consumption tax; and whether it does or not, aggregate saving should increase. Most pension funds will probably remove restrictions and penalties on early withdrawals. But with this removal, employer contributions to pension funds may increase. After all, administrative convenience will continue to give an advantage to employer-financed pension funds over individual saving. Today, employees are reluctant to have too much of their wealth "locked up" in a pension fund until retirement, and this reluctance limits employer contributions. But with restrictions and penalties removed, employees may request larger pension contributions. Preretirement withdrawals may increase. But it is quite possible that an increase in contributions will outweigh any increase in withdrawals.

More generally, households today must be willing to have their wealth locked up until retirement in order to obtain a tax advantage for saving. Under a personal consumption tax, households will be able to obtain a tax advantage for saving without locking up their wealth.

Households may withdraw more wealth prior to retirement. But they will accumulate more wealth in the first place. It seems likely that the increase in gross saving will exceed any increase in withdrawals so that aggregate saving will increase.

Today, private investment funds advertise tax-favored saving vehicles, and this probably increases saving among alert households despite the fact that these vehicles are generally subject to "lock-up." Some analysts (Steurle 1996; Bernheim 1996) note that such advertising would be ended by conversion to a personal consumption tax; they wonder whether this would reduce aggregate saving. But the termination of private advertising would be replaced by public "advertising" that reaches virtually every household: the household tax return with its saving deduction. Moreover, the IRS would be promoting a superior "product": a saving deduction without "lock-up." Its promotional message would be simpler: "Any saving in any form in any amount for any duration is tax deductible." The improvement of the saving "product," the simplicity of the message, and the greater coverage of IRS "advertising," are all likely to increase aggregate saving.

Raising the Saving Rate without Causing a Recession

Economists agree that increasing our saving rate will achieve higher output and consumption per person in the long run. But the increase must be phased in gradually to avoid a temporary recession (Seidman 1990b, chapter 2; Lewis and Seidman 1994). Here's an illustration of how it can be done.

Today, output, consumption, and investment all normally grow about 2.5% per year, investment (private plus public) is roughly 20% of output, and consumption (private plus public) is roughly 80%. Envision a half-decade transition. During the half decade, our aim is to keep output growing about 2.5% while gradually raising the share of output that consists of investment goods (for example, to 24%) while gradually reducing the share that consists of consumer goods (for example, to 76%). This will happen if consumer goods production grows about 1.5% per year while investment goods production grows a little over 6% per year.[1] From then on, consumer goods and investment goods can grow at the same rate—a rate that will be a bit faster than 2.5% for many years because of the higher capital stock that is achieved by fast investment growth during the half decade.

Notice several things about this half-decade transition. Consumer goods production maintains a positive growth rate (1.5% per year), a point below normal. Although there may be a modest rise in layoffs in the consumer goods sector, the growth slowdown will mainly be handled by voluntary quits and retirements. At the same time, job openings will expand rapidly in the investment goods sector. These will be filled by persons shifting voluntarily or involuntarily out of the consumer goods sector and by new entrants to the labor force.

During the half decade, a phased conversion to the USA Tax (or any other consumption tax) should induce the slower consumption growth, and the Federal Reserve would induce the faster investment growth. The Fed does it by reducing interest rates enough to induce business managers to step up their orders of investment goods, thereby stimulating faster investment goods production. Total demand (consumption plus investment) and hence total output will continue to grow at its normal 2.5%, thereby maintaining a constant unemployment rate and avoiding recession.

Thus, to avoid a recession during the transition to a permanently higher saving rate, it is important to gradually phase in the USA Tax (or any other consumption tax), so consumption growth declines modestly for roughly a half decade but always remains positive. Methods for implementing a gradual phase-in of the USA Tax are discussed in chapter 4.

Should We Enact the USA Tax?

Here's what a USA Tax advocate might say: "Look at the tables again. The United States is a low-saving country. Part of the reason is a set of distortions that have discouraged saving. At stake is our future standard of living and our relative economic position in the world. If the USA Tax meets the tests of fairness and practicality, it deserves serious consideration." These two issues are addressed in the next two chapters.

3   Fairness

USA Tax advocates argue that what distinguishes the USA Tax is that it both encourages saving and has a strong claim to fairness. They contend that other consumption taxes are unfair though they encourage saving, and that the income tax discourages saving though it also has a strong claim to fairness. Not surprisingly, advocates of other consumption taxes contend they are fair, while income tax proponents minimize any discouragement of saving and assert that it is the fairest tax. But before discussing the fairness of alternative taxes, some interesting facts about the current distribution of the tax burden and the recent rise in U.S. earnings inequality need to be considered.

The Current Distribution of the Tax Burden

Table 3.1 shows how pretax income is distributed among families. Look at the bottom three rows of the 1990 column. In 1990 the richest 10% received 36.1% of the nation's pretax income; the richest 5%, 25.7%; and the richest 1%, 12.8%. What income levels did it take to make it to each pretax income class? To make the numbers more meaningful for citizens in the mid-1990s, a projection for 1996 is given. To be in the richest 10% in 1996 requires an income of at least $108,704; in the richest 5%, $145,412; in the richest 1%, $349,438.

It should of course be recognized that some of the low-quintile families have low income in a given year simply because they are young or old. But many who grow up in inner-city neighborhoods have modest incomes all their lives. Similarly, there are a few people who spend only a few years in the richest brackets, spending the rest of their lives in modest brackets (for example, the athlete who manages to play only a year or two in the National Basketball Association or National Football

Table 3.1
Shares of pretax income for all families (%)

All families (by income group)	1980	1985	1990	Income threshold in 1996(projected)
Lowest quintile	4.5	3.8	3.7	0
Second quintile	10.3	9.4	9.2	15,604
Middle quintile	15.5	14.7	14.5	29,717
Fourth quintile	22.5	21.9	21.7	48,660
Highest quintile	47.5	50.7	51.4	79,056
	100.0	100.0	100.0	
Top 10 percent	31.7	35.0	36.1	108,704
Top 5 percent	21.4	24.5	25.7	145,412
Top 1 percent	9.4	11.8	12.8	349,438

Sources: 1993 Green Book (Committee on Ways and Means, U.S. House of Representatives, which cites source as Congressional Budget Office [CBO]) table 17, p. 1506 for three left columns; U.S. Treasury, Office of Tax Analysis (1996, p. 455) for right column.

League). But many of the rich are affluent most of their lives—they are business executives, physicians, lawyers, and so on. Just take a drive through an affluent neighborhood. How many residents will soon move to a nonaffluent neighborhood? Not many.

Table 3.1 also shows that pretax income inequality significantly increased during the 1980s. From 1980 to 1990, the share of each quintile except the top declined, while the share of the top quintile rose from 47.5% to 51.4%; the top 10%, from 31.7% to 36.1%; the top 5%, from 21.4% to 25.7%; and the top 1%, from 9.4% to 12.8%.

Given this substantial permanent, lifetime inequality in pretax incomes, it is not surprising that Congress has deemed it fair to make the federal tax system progressive, taking a greater percentage from the affluent than from moderate-income households. Because the other major federal tax, the Social Security payroll tax, is regressive—with the same rate for all employees up to a ceiling ($61,200 in 1995) and then zero for income above the ceiling—significant graduation in the household income tax schedule is required to achieve progressivity in federal taxes.

Table 3.2 shows the effective (average) tax rate (the ratio of federal taxes to income) that Congress has achieved in selected years for different income groups. The ratio includes all federal taxes. Of course, the highest tax rate an affluent household pays on its last $100 of income— its "marginal tax rate"—exceeds its effective tax rate because it pays

Table 3.2
Total federal effective tax rates for all families (%)

All families (by income group)	1980	1985	1990	1994b	1994a
Lowest quintile	8.1	10.4	8.9	7.0	5.0
Second quintile	15.6	15.9	15.8	15.0	14.9
Middle quintile	19.8	19.2	19.5	19.3	19.5
Fourth quintile	22.9	21.7	22.1	22.1	22.3
Highest quintile	27.6	24.1	25.5	26.2	27.9
Top 10 percent	28.7	24.4	26.0	27.0	29.2
Top 5 percent	29.7	24.4	26.2	27.4	30.4
Top 1 percent	31.9	24.5	26.3	28.0	33.2
Overall	23.3	21.8	22.6	22.8	23.7

Note: Column 1994b is projection before 1993 tax act (OBRA-1993); column 1994a is projection after 1993 tax act.
Sources: 1993 Green Book (Committee on Ways and Means, U.S. House of Representatives, which cites source as CBO), table 11, p. 1497 for three left columns; Congressional Budget Office (1994, p. 32) for two right columns.

lower rates on most of its income. Thus a high-income person in 1985 was in a "50% tax bracket" for labor income, interest, and dividends (though not capital gains)—the last $100 earned was taxed 50%—but the average tax rate did not exceed 25%. Note that the 1993 tax act raised the tax rate of the very affluent several points (for example, from 28.0% to 33.2% for the richest 1%). Although these effective tax rates are much lower than the marginal bracket rates, they do succeed in raising substantial revenue from the affluent, as is evident from table 3.3.

The conclusion to be drawn from table 3.3 is that despite the various tax preferences of the current income tax and the services of tax lawyers and accountants, most of the affluent pay substantial federal taxes. In 1990, the richest 10% paid 41.6% of federal taxes; the richest 5%, 29.8%, and the richest 1%, 14.9%. Because the payroll tax is proportional up to the $61,200 ceiling (1995) and regressive beyond it, the primary cause of these large affluent tax shares is clearly the graduated rate schedule of the household income tax.

It is sometimes argued that there is no point trying to raise much revenue from the rich. It is claimed that their income is too small a share of national income, and that they employ clever accountants and lawyers to make sure they pay little or no tax. Tables 3.1 and 3.3 demonstrate emphatically how wrong these assertions are. Table 3.1 shows that the top 10% get over a third of the nation's income; the top

Table 3.3
Shares of total federal taxes paid by all families (%)

All families (by income group)	1980	1985	1990	1994b
Lowest quintile	1.6	1.8	1.4	1.1
Second quintile	6.9	6.9	6.4	6.1
Middle quintile	13.2	13.0	12.5	12.4
Fourth quintile	22.1	21.9	21.2	20.9
Highest quintile	56.2	56.2	58.2	59.2
	100.0	100.0	100.0	100.0
Top 10 percent	39.1	39.2	41.6	42.7
Top 5 percent	27.4	27.5	29.8	31.0
Top 1 percent	12.8	13.3	14.9	15.8

Note: Column 1994b is projection before 1993 tax act (OBRA-1993).
Source: 1993 Green Book (Committee on Ways and Means, U.S. House of Representatives, which cites source as CBO), table 25, p. 1515.

5% get about a fourth; and the top 1% about an eighth. These are large shares. But can the government collect much tax revenue from them? Table 3.3 gives an unequivocal answer: it can indeed.

In fact, these tax shares may seem so large that it provokes the question: Is the affluent share of after-income much lower than its share of before-tax income? Table 3.4 shows that the answer is no. After the graduated income tax has done its work, their share is almost as great. The share of 1990 after-tax income is 34.5% for the top 10% (compared with 36.1% of pretax income in table 3.1); 24.5% for the top 5% (versus 25.7% of pretax income); and 12.2% for the top 1% (versus 12.8% of pretax income). Although the 1993 tax act (OBRA) probably reduced affluent after-tax income shares a little further, the key fact remains: despite the graduated income tax, the affluent's share of after-tax income is only a few percentage points less than its share of pretax income.

Summarizing the four tables, there is substantial inequality in the pretax distribution of income, and it significantly increased in the 1980s. Using average tax rates that do not exceed 33%, the federal tax system succeeds in raising substantial revenue from the affluent. Because the payroll tax is proportional up to its ceiling ($61,200 in 1995) and regressive beyond, the key to raising revenue from the affluent is clearly the graduated tax rate schedule of the household income tax. Despite various preferences in the current income tax and the services of tax lawyers and accountants, the affluent pay a large share of total federal taxes. Yet the affluent get almost as large a share of after-tax income as

Table 3.4
Shares of after-tax income for all families (%)

All families (by income group)	1980	1985	1990
Lowest quintile	5.4	4.4	4.3
Second quintile	11.4	10.1	10.0
Middle quintile	16.2	15.2	15.1
Fourth quintile	22.6	21.9	21.8
Highest quintile	44.9	49.2	49.5
	100.0	100.0	100.0
Top 10 percent	29.5	33.8	34.5
Top 5 percent	19.6	23.7	24.5
Top 1 percent	8.3	11.3	12.2

Source: 1993 Green Book (Committee on Ways and Means, U.S. House of Representatives, which cites source as CBO), table 18, p. 1507.

pretax income. These crucial facts should be borne in mind as we discuss the fairness of alternative tax reforms.

Rising U.S. Income Inequality

A search for the causes of rising U.S. income inequality has engaged the efforts of numerous economists in recent years and generated controversy and disagreement. But on one point most experts agree. As Burtless writes (1996, pp. 28–29):

There is no disputing the worsening trend in U.S. income inequality.... Between 1969 and 1993, real [inflation-adjusted] earnings fell for men in the bottom 40 percent of the earnings distribution, remained unchanged for men in the middle quintile, and rose for men at the top. The disparate trends in wage earnings became more pronounced after 1979.... Although overall wage trends have been much healthier for women, women have also experienced widening earnings disparities, especially in recent years. After 1979 women in the top quintile saw their earnings climb more than 25 percent. For women at the bottom, annual earnings fell after 1979.

Levy and Murnane (1992, p. 1333) begin their survey of recent trends in earnings inequality as follows:

From the perspective of 1991, U.S. earnings trends since 1950 are demarcated by two years: 1973 and 1979. Nineteen-hundred-seventy-three marked the end of rapid real earnings growth and the beginning of slower growth bordering on stagnation. Nineteen-hundred-seventy-nine marked the beginning of a sharp acceleration in the growth of earnings inequality, particularly among men.

Gottschalk (1993, pp. 136, 141) draws this conclusion from data on seven economically advanced countries:

It is now widely recognized that earnings inequality grew rapidly in the United States during the 1970s and 1980s.... In summary, the increase in inequality of earnings was not limited to the United States. While the United States had the largest increase in inequality of earnings, all other countries in this study also experienced increases in inequality.

What has caused this rising inequality? Burtless (1996, pp. 10–11) writes:

Among economists, the leading explanation for increased wage inequality is changes in the technology of production. Such innovations as the personal computer or new forms of business organization have favored workers with greater skill and reduced the value of unskilled labor.But other developments are also at work. Economic deregulation, new patterns of immigration into the United States, declining minimum wages, and the dwindling influence of labor unions have also contributed to the job woes of unskilled and semi-skilled workers. Liberal trade with the newly industrializing countries of the world has certainly played a part in worsening the job prospects of America's unskilled workers.

As we consider the fairness of alternative taxes, it will be important to keep in mind the recent trend of rising inequality of earnings.

The National Sales Tax and the VAT

Now consider the proposal to replace the individual and corporate income taxes with a national sales tax or a value-added tax (VAT). April 15 would be just another day. No household would ever report its income or consumption to the Internal Revenue Service, so the IRS would no longer audit households. It is crucial to recognize that the tax system would no longer be a vehicle for scaling assistance according to a household's income or consumption. For example, the refundable earned income tax credit (EITC), which sends government checks to households with low-wage income, would be automatically terminated.

When the debate turns to fairness, national sales tax advocates are asked to address the fact that as we move from low- to high-income households in a given year, the percentage of income saved generally rises—equivalently, the percentage consumed falls. After the population has rung up the cash registers this year, those who have high incomes will pay a smaller percentage of their income in sales tax than those who have low incomes. This strikes many (though not all) citizens as unfair if the sales tax is to become our largest source of federal revenue.

Sales taxers reply that one year's data are misleading. They point out that some people with low income this year are young or retired, so their average income over a lifetime is much higher; and many people with high income this year are middle-aged at the peak of their earnings and the peak of their propensity to save, so their average income over their lifetime is much lower. Sales taxers argue that with their tax the young and old pay a high tax percentage while the middle-aged pay a low tax percentage, so it evens out over a lifetime. Over a whole lifetime, many people will consume their entire income and pay about the same percentage under a sales tax.

But what about the very affluent who keep saving substantial percentages right up to their death? They will consume less than their entire income over their lifetime, leave substantial gifts and bequests to heirs, and hence pay a smaller percentage than others under a sales tax. Thus some sales taxers are wrong when they claim that everyone eventually consumes—and hence pays sales tax—on his entire lifetime income. Some of the very affluent consume less than their lifetime income.

But even if these sales taxers were right, the basic question remains: Is it fair for the affluent to pay the same percentage of lifetime income as moderate- and low-income people? Most citizens apparently don't think so. Although Congress has always been free to set the single rate for everyone under the income tax, it never has. Rates have always been set much higher for the affluent. The same has been true in virtually all other economically advanced countries. A majority of citizens apparently believe that the affluent should pay a higher percentage than the middle class, who in turn should pay a higher percentage than low-income working households.[1]

A value-added tax is really a sales tax that is partly collected at each stage of production rather than solely at the final retail stage (McLure 1987). Under a VAT, the firm takes its sales revenue and subtracts purchases from other firms, including investment goods. Thus a VAT taxes output (value-added) minus investment, which equals consumption. It is this deduction of investment goods that makes a VAT a consumption tax.

A VAT is utilized by most other economically advanced countries in addition to, not instead of, a personal income tax. Similarly, the business component of the USA Tax is a VAT that replaces the corporate income tax, but does not replace the personal tax (the USA VAT is implemented by the subtraction method, while the European VAT is implemented by the credit-invoice method). The USA Tax will raise most of its revenue from its household tax, not its business tax. In this chapter on fairness, we consider only a "replacement VAT" that is intended to replace the household tax, not supplement it.

As a replacement, the VAT has the same problem as the sales tax. Even if the affluent eventually consume all their lifetime income, they will pay the same percentage of lifetime income as low-income people. And if an affluent household consumes less than its lifetime income, leaving substantial gifts and bequests to heirs, then it will pay a lower percentage. Hence the replacement VAT will again be judged unfair by a majority of citizens.

In 1995, the Office of Tax Analysis of the U.S. Treasury used its tax model to simulate the impact of a flat-rate consumption tax (retail sales or value-added). Deputy Assistant Secretary of the U.S. Treasury for Tax Analysis, Eric Toder, supervised the simulation and presented the results in testimony before the Senate Budget Committee on February 22. The simulation results (revised on March 7), presented in table 3.5, show the distributional effect of replacing the revenue of the corporate and personal income taxes (including the earned income tax credit) with a general single-rate consumption tax with no exemptions.

For the top 10%, repeal of the income (Y) tax raises after-tax income $427.7 billion (column 2), while the flat-rate consumption tax reduces after-tax income only $264.9 billion (column 3), so after-tax income increases $162.8 billion (column 4), or 8.6% (column 5). For the top 5%, after-tax income increases 11.7%; for the top 1%, 17.7%. The most startling result is shown in the right column, which indicates that the richest 1% would have their taxes cut in half, and that all quintiles except the top would suffer a tax increase. In light of the recent widening inequality of wage earnings and income, will anyone step forward and argue that this redistribution of the tax burden is fair?

To address this problem, sales tax and VAT advocates often propose exemptions for certain categories of goods such as food. This is the standard approach for state sales taxes and European VATs. But it is not very satisfactory.

Kay and King (1990, pp. 99–100) explain:

A common objection to the imposition of indirect taxes [sales tax or VAT] is that they take no account of an individual's personal circumstances, and indeed are

Table 3.5
Replace current individual and corporate income taxes (including the EITC) with a 14.5% flat rate consumption tax with no exemptions (1996 income levels)

Family economic income quintile	After-tax income under current law	Change in after-tax income				Percent change in federal taxes
		Repeal Y-tax	C-tax	Total change	Percent change	
Lowest	171.1	−4.5	−14.5	−19.0	−11.1	134.1
Second	431.0	9.9	−53.1	−43.2	−10.0	70.5
Third	697.9	59.6	−100.6	−40.9	−5.9	27.9
Fourth	1,091.9	126.6	−168.8	−42.2	−3.9	15.5
Highest	2,693.1	536.7	−391.4	145.4	5.4	−18.6
Total	5,054.7	729.4	−729.4	0.0	0.0	0.0
Top 10%	1,899.8	427.7	−264.9	162.8	8.6	−28.8
Top 5%	1,371.5	341.2	−180.5	160.7	11.7	−38.7
Top 1%	683.5	202.7	−81.5	121.2	17.7	−54.6

Source: This is a March 7, 1995, revision of table 1 (dated February 14, 1995) on p. 21 of Toder's testimony.

often, though not always, regressive. What progressivity does exist is achieved by taxing at higher rates of VAT or excise duties those commodities that are consumed relatively more by the rich than by the poor. Since consumption patterns vary between individuals this is a rather arbitrary and haphazard method of redistribution, which is a blessing to the rich man who loves plain cooking and reading, and hard on the poor man who rejects conventional standards of attire and nutrition and adopts consumption patterns more usually associated with the rich.... It is important to realize that this objection cannot be levelled at an expenditure [personal consumption] tax that is a tax on the total value of an individual's expenditure in the course of a year. In itself it does not discriminate between consumption on different commodities, and can be as progressive as desired in exactly the same way an income tax is progressive.

Fisher and Fisher (1942, p. 5) explain why a personal consumption ("spendings") tax offers a better way to exempt "necessities":

THE TAX WOULD BE A LUXURY TAX

It will be seen that our proposed new income tax is not merely a spendings tax; it is practically a luxury-spendings tax—"luxury" being defined as any excess above reasonable necessities. These necessities would mostly escape the tax through the "minimum exemptions." Thus, unlike a sales tax, this luxury tax would allow little or no taxing of necessities; and would spare the spendings of the very poor. The middle class and the rich would bear the burden; for, the greater the spendings—which means the more luxurious—the higher the rate.

Such a luxury-spendings tax is more truly a luxury tax than any excise tax on specific luxuries, such as costly automobiles, opera tickets, or Oriental rugs. To define satisfactorily specific objects as "luxuries" is impossible; but to measure satisfactorily what constitutes luxurious spending, and with definite gradations, is easy.

Graetz (1980, p. 162) amplifies the Fishers' point:

The principal difficulties with the value-added tax and the sales tax are precisely those that a well-designed expenditure [personal consumption] tax should avoid. First, value-added and retail sales taxes are invariably imposed on less than a full consumption base.... Second, value-added or retail sales taxes are not related to a person's total amount of consumption. An expenditure tax should avoid the narrowing of the tax base that inevitably seems to accompany value-added or sales taxes and would achieve individualization of the tax burden by imposing a tax on a consumption base at progressive rates directly related to a person's overall level of consumption.

Some sales tax and VAT advocates have proposed a cash rebate to reduce the burden on low-income households. But note that the rebate must be given to all households because there is no longer any household tax to provide information about each household's income or consumption. For example, every household might be mailed $1,000 per adult and $500 per child. Because the rebate is the same regardless of family income, it would offset a larger percentage of the sales tax or VAT burden for low-income households than for high-income households.

But is a universal rebate practical? To mail every U.S. household a check scaled to the number in the household would be unprecedented. Presumably Social Security numbers would be used to try to assure that each person receives only one payment. Remember, April 15 household tax returns cannot be used because they have been abolished. Could fraud be contained to a tolerable level? Recently, there has been concern about fraud under the earned income tax credit (EITC) where only a relatively small percentage of the U.S. population are mailed checks. Although progress is being made to reduce EITC fraud (in part by using Social Security numbers), the task would be much more difficult for the entire U.S. population.

Some futuristic advocates have suggested that a universal rebate could be implemented by issuing every U.S. household a special credit card instead of a check. At the cash register, tax would be imposed only if the electronic card shows that card purchases have exceeded $10,000 that year. But it's not obvious whether this would be less subject to fraud.

The crucial point, however, is this: Even if a universal rebate, or the special credit card, were administratively feasible, the sales tax or VAT would still be much less progressive than the current income tax. Thus the rebate or special card would not satisfy any citizen who believes that a fair tax should have the affluent bear a significantly greater percentage burden than the nonaffluent. As we have seen, apparently the majority of Americans hold this view.

The Flat Tax

At first glance, the flat tax looks different from a sales tax or a VAT because it retains a household tax return that must be filed on April 15. Like the USA Tax, the flat tax has two components: a business tax and a household tax. Its business tax is a subtraction VAT except that cash wage payments are deductible (recall that a VAT does not permit a deduction for wages, only for purchases from other firms). But its architects, Stanford economist Robert Hall and Hoover Institute fellow Alvin Rabushka, explain that the flat tax is similar to a VAT, and they are right. They advise that the best way to understand their flat tax is to begin with its business tax:

Here is the logic of our system, stripped to basics: We want to tax consumption. The public does one of two things with its income—spends it or invests it. We can measure consumption as income minus investment. A really simple tax would just have each firm pay tax on the total amount of income generated by the firm less that firm's investment in plant and equipment. The value-added tax works just that way. But a value-added tax is unfair because it is not progressive. That's why we break the tax in two. The firm pays tax on all the income generated at the firm except the income paid to its workers. The workers pay tax on what they earn, and the tax they pay is progressive. (Hall and Rabushka 1995, p. 55)

So we can think of the flat tax this way. Imagine initially abolishing the household tax, just as the sales tax or replacement VAT would. Then imagine replacing the corporate income tax with a 20% VAT. Now make one change: let the firms deduct cash wages and make households pay a 20% tax on wage income. If a household were taxed on its entire wage income, it can be shown that this one change would make no difference.[2] But the flat tax lets the household take a generous family allowance on its tax return. If the allowance is $30,000 for a family of four, then the family with $20,000 of wage income pays no tax (instead of \$4,000).[3] Thanks to the allowance, its flat tax burden is \$4,000 less than it would be under the VAT.

Although the flat tax family allowance helps low-wage families, another feature harms these families: the termination of the earned income tax credit (EITC). Because the flat tax has a household return for wage income, it could retain the EITC. But it doesn't. The flat tax terminates all deductions and credits to keep its tax rate as low as possible and to ensure that it fits on a postcard. But the EITC currently makes substantial payments to households with low-wage income. By contrast, the USA Tax not only retains the EITC, but also introduces a new payroll tax credit.

The most striking feature of the flat tax, however, is its impact on the affluent. Here it is interesting to consult Hall and Rabushka's first flat tax book, in which they make this remarkable concession:

The simple [flat] tax is not immediately a good deal for most Americans. Unless the tax improves the performance of the economy, it will let a minority of high-income families off the hook for the very high taxes they are now paying and finance the move by slightly raising everybody else's taxes. (Hall and Rabushka 1983, p. 53)

After arguing that in the long run everyone will benefit when everyone works harder and saves more in response to lower marginal tax rates, they make another striking admission (p. 58):

Now for some bad news. The simple tax does not make everybody better off straight away. Heavy taxation of successful people yields quite a bit of revenue, as well as pushing them out of their most productive undertakings and diverting their attention to tax avoidance. Until a response to improved incentives takes place, it is an obvious mathematical law that lower taxes on the successful will have to be made up by higher taxes on average people.

After repeating their assertion that everyone will benefit in the long run, they write (p. 58):

Because the critics of the flat tax have already made a big point about their calculations of who wins and who loses when taxes are reformed, we will spend some time on the issue. The first thing to say is that the critics are right on their own ground. If incomes remain exactly the same after tax reform, then the poor and the middle class subsidize the rich. Though all calculations of this kind are full of questions and uncertainties, no matter how we do it, we reach the same general conclusion. Tax reform is not immediately a good thing for the majority.

Once again, they emphasize their belief that everyone will benefit in the long run.

Two points are worth noting about these remarkable paragraphs. First, Hall and Rabushka admit that although the flat tax initially hurts ordinary people, it immediately helps the rich. Second, they are fond of calling the rich "successful." Thus there is little doubt that the flat tax immediately rewards "the successful," and asks the less successful to wait patiently, comforted by the promise that they will eventually escape its immediate burden.

Just two years later, however, Hall and Rabushka (1985) issued a second flat tax book with an intriguing preface. In it, they retract their concessions of 1983. They explain (pp. viii–ix):

Our case for the proposal has changed a great deal. Probably most important is our demonstration that the existing tax system is severely biased against wages and salaries. Earlier, we were defensive about a tax structure that appeared to give more relief to higher reported incomes than to middle incomes. Now we see that the issue is not what happens in terms of reported income, but hidden income. A great deal of the income received by the wealthy is untaxed because it takes the form of business income, which the current system taxes least successfully. By putting an effective tax on business income, we would shift the burden of taxation away from wage and salary earners and toward the prosperous recipients of business income. Some people interpreted the earlier book as saying that we should sacrifice a little fairness for the sake of a more efficient economy. Now we contend that fairness and efficiency can be achieved as part of the same reform.

Their 1985 argument is based on the allegation that many affluent households are paying little tax now under the income tax. How much legal avoidance and illegal evasion occurs among the affluent has been subject to some study and much speculation. But table 3.3 strikingly demonstrates that a large share of federal tax revenue is paid by affluent households under the current income tax: in 1994 the richest 10% paid over 40% of federal tax; the richest 5% about 30%; and the richest 1% about 15%. It is not true that the current income tax allows the affluent to pay a small share of taxes.

In the January 22, 1996, issue of *Tax Notes*, the Office of Tax Analysis (OTA) of the U.S. Treasury presents an analysis of the revenue and distributional impact of the flat tax. Initially, OTA analyzes the July 1995 flat tax proposal of Representative Dick Armey (R-Texas) and Senator Richard Shelby (R-Alabama), which contains a 17% tax rate on households and business net cash flow, an allowance of $21,400 for joint filers, and an additional deduction of $5,000 for each dependent—hence, a $31,400 deduction for a family of four.

Table 3.6
Replace current individual and corporate income taxes (including the EITC) with a revenue-neutral 20.8% flat rate tax (1996 income levels)

Family economic income quintile	After-tax income under current law	Change in after-tax income				Percent change in federal taxes
		Repeal Y-tax	Flat tax	Total change	Percent change	
Lowest	171.1	–4.5	–7.0	–11.5	–6.7	80.9
Second	431.0	9.9	–33.0	–23.1	–5.4	37.7
Third	697.9	59.6	–79.7	–20.1	–2.9	13.7
Fourth	1,091.9	126.6	–153.3	–26.7	–2.4	9.8
Highest	2,693.1	536.7	–479.4	57.3	2.1	–7.4
Total	5,054.7	729.4	–753.8	–24.4	–0.5	1.9
Top 10%	1,899.8	427.7	–348.8	78.9	4.2	–14.0
Top 5%	1,371.5	341.2	–252.8	88.4	6.4	–21.3
Top 1%	683.5	202.7	–122.6	80.1	11.7	–36.1

Source: U.S. Treasury, Office of Tax Analysis (1996, p. 455). See endnote 5 for further details.

OTA estimates that in 1996 this flat tax would raise only about 80% as much revenue as the income tax it replaces.[4] Because income tax revenue is about 10% of GDP, this would cause tax revenue to fall 2% of GDP, so federal tax revenue would fall from 19% of GDP to 17%. With federal spending 22% of GDP, the federal budget deficit would rise from 3% of GDP to 5%—the budget deficit would rise roughly 67% (2%/3%).

What tax rate would it take for a flat tax with a $31,400 deduction to raise the same revenue as the income tax? About 21%, estimates OTA. OTA then analyzes the distributional impact of this 21% revenue-neutral flat tax, presented in table 3.6.[5] For the top 10%, repeal of the income (Y) tax raises after-tax income $427.7 billion (column 2), while the flat tax reduces after-tax income only $348.8 billion (column 3), so after-tax income increases $78.9 billion (column 4), or 4.2% (column 5). For the top 5%, after-tax income increases 6.4%, while for the top 1%, after-tax income increases 11.7%.

The public might be concerned about the figures in the right column, which indicate that the top 1% (income over $349,438) enjoy a 36% tax cut; the top 5% (income over $145,412) a 21% tax cut; and the top 10% (income over $108,704) a 14% tax cut. And all quintiles except the top suffer a tax increase, while the bottom quintile (income under $15,604) suffers an 81% tax increase. In light of the recent widening inequality of wage earnings and income, will anyone step forward and argue that this redistribution of the tax burden is fair?

It's not hard to understand how the affluent get a large tax cut: the top rate is 20.8%, compared to 39.6% under the current income tax. Because it raises the same total revenue as the income tax, the 20.8% flat tax must raise taxes on the nonaffluent. But exactly how does the flat tax make the nonaffluent pay more? For low-income working families, removal of the earned income credit is one important reason. The OTA gives the example of a married couple earning $17,680 (twice the minimum wage) with two children. In 1996 the flat tax would terminate an earned income credit of $2,278. According to OTA, together with other adjustments, this family would end up $2,442 worse off due to the flat tax.

For middle-class families, ending the employer's deduction for health insurance and FICA (Social Security and Medicare) contributions is often the key. The OTA gives an example of a married couple earning $50,000 plus an employer health insurance contribution of $4,950. The employer makes a FICA contribution of $3,825 (7.65% of $50,000). With a 20.82% flat tax, terminating the deduction costs the employer 20.82% x ($4,950 + $3,825) or $1,827. OTA assumes that this $1,827 burden is eventually shifted to the employee through a lower salary.[6] According to OTA, together with other adjustments, this family would end up $1,604 worse off due to the flat tax.

True, the flat tax meets the technical definition of "progressivity." The flat tax has some progressivity because it really has two tax rates, not one: 0% on the first $30,000 (approximately) of wage income, and a 20% (approximately) rate on all additional income. With two rates, the ratio of tax to income rises from 0% for low-income households to 20% for the very rich; and a rising ratio implies that the flat tax is "progressive."

Of course, the real issue is the degree of progressivity. With a 20% flat tax, the ratio of tax to income will never exceed 20% no matter how rich the household. By contrast, under the current income tax, the ratio approaches 40% for a very rich household. The U.S. Treasury's OTA table just presented shows that the current income tax achieves a much higher tax burden on the affluent than the mildly progressive flat tax. By contrast, the designers of the USA Tax have instructed technicians to determine a set of rates and brackets for the USA Tax that will achieve roughly the same distribution of the tax burden as the current income tax.

The OTA study has not gone unchallenged. Flat tax advocates assert that the OTA study is flawed because it uses "static analysis"—it assumes that the supplies of labor and capital will be unresponsive to a cut in tax rates.[7] They argue that lower marginal tax rates will induce many to supply more labor and capital (saving) to the economy; hence, a tax rate of 17% will raise enough revenue, contrary to OTA's assumption that a 21% rate is required. In particular, the affluent will contribute at least as much revenue with a 17% rate as currently, not only because they will supply more labor and capital, but also because they will reduce their tax avoidance activities.

Most economists agree that flat taxers are right, in principle, to insist that supply-side effects be taken into account. However, most doubt that actual supply-side responses would be large enough to reverse the likely headline that emerges from the OTA's static analysis: "The flat tax significantly redistributes the tax burden from the affluent to the nonaffluent."

Finally, some flat tax supporters do not dispute the headline. In fact, they regard such a redistribution as fair. They believe the current tax burden should be shifted away from the affluent because, in their view, the affluent have been overtaxed. Hall and Rabushka believe that "successful people" have been penalized for their effort and achievement. To these flat taxers, a mildly progressive tax—the flat tax—is fairer than a significantly progressive tax, such as the current income tax or the proposed USA Tax.

In reply, those who would retain the current degree of progressivity of the household tax make two points. First, it offsets the regressivity of the payroll tax. Second, as table 3.4 shows, despite the current graduated income tax, the share of 1990 after-tax national income is 34.5% for the top 10% (compared with 36.1% of pretax income in table 3.1); 24.5% for the top 5% (versus 25.7% of pretax income); and 12.2% for the top 1% (versus 12.8% of pretax income). The current degree of progressivity leaves the affluent with a large share of the nation's after-tax income—almost as large as its share of pretax income.

A Progressive Income Tax versus a Progressive Consumption Tax

Like the income tax, the USA Tax utilizes graduated rates so it can be every bit as progressive as any income tax. The USA Tax can therefore raise the same proportion of tax revenue from high- , middle- , and low-income households as the income tax. To see this, suppose the affluent save 20%, the middle class 10%, and low-income people 0%. If an unlimited savings allowance were introduced, but Congress foolishly forgot to change the tax rates in the tax table, then of course the affluent would enjoy a large tax cut, the middle class a moderate cut, and low-income people none at all. But then there would also be a huge drop in federal tax revenue, making our budget deficit problem even worse.

The USA Tax is designed to raise the same total revenue as the current income tax. To raise the same dollars, tax rates must be raised in response to the new saving deduction. How should the rates be raised? Clearly, to get the same dollars from the affluent, in this illustration rates for the affluent must be raised roughly 20% to offset the 20% saving deduction; roughly 10% will do the trick for the middle class; and no change in rates will be needed for low-income households. That's what the USA Tax will do. The percentages will be higher in order to keep the dollars the same.

The graduated USA Tax will distribute the tax burden across classes the same as the graduated income tax. Of course, within each class some will do better and others worse: affluent high savers will pay less tax, affluent low savers, more tax; the average affluent household will pay the same tax. Thus if a citizen favors significant graduation, that is indeed a reason to prefer the income tax to the sales tax, the VAT, and the flat tax. But it is not a reason to prefer the income tax to the USA Tax.

So is it fairer, using graduated rates, to tax a person according to his consumption rather than his income? Income tax advocates say "no," for one basic reason: they claim that income is a better measure of ability to pay than consumption. Consider a miser with high income but low consumption. Isn't it fairer, say income tax advocates, to levy a high tax on the miser, whose ability to pay is high, rather than a low tax simply because he chooses to consume little? Excellent expositions of the fairness case for an income tax include Goode (1980) and Pechman (1990). Because these arguments have been made many times and are widely known, I will concentrate here on the arguments made by advocates of a progressive consumption tax.

The basic proposition of progressive consumption tax proponents is this: It is fairer to tax a person according to what he takes out of the economic pie, rather than according to what he contributes to it.

A person's income often (but not always) roughly reflects that person's production—the contribution to economic output. Hence a tax on income is roughly a tax on a person's contribution to the economic pie.

By contrast, a tax on consumption is a tax on the slice of the pie that a person withdraws for his own satisfaction.

When a person produces and earns income, a contribution is made to the pool of available goods and services. Production adds, rather than subtracts, from others' economic well-being. Income is a potential claim to goods, not the actual withdrawal of goods. But when people actually withdraw resources for their own consumption, then these resources are not available for others to consume; nor are the resources available for firms to invest in plant, equipment, and technology, thereby raising everyone's productivity and earnings in the future. Progressive consumption tax proponents argue that it is fairer to charge each person, through tax, according to what he subtracts from what is available to others, rather than what he adds to what is available.

Consider Carl and Susan. They have the same production and income, but Carl uses his entire income to withdraw goods for his own enjoyment, while Susan uses only a fraction of her income to withdraw consumption goods, leaving resources for others to consume and invest. Is it really fair to tax them equally? Both have the power to consume equally. But Susan leaves more for others than Carl.

According to this view of fairness, Carl should pay more tax than Susan. But suppose Carl consumes twice as much as Susan. Does this mean he should pay exactly twice as much tax? Not at all. Advocates of a progressive consumption tax believe that Carl should pay more than twice the tax that Susan pays. But the base of the tax should be consumption, not income.

Let there be no misunderstanding: Consumption is neither wrong nor harmful. My argument is simply that when a person consumes, he leaves less resources for others, so it seems fair to charge the person according to his withdrawal of resources. And it surely seems fairer than charging a person according to the income he earns (roughly reflecting the output he contributes), whether or not he subtracts much or little from what is available for others.

In their path-breaking monograph advocating a progressive consumption ("spendings") tax, *Constructive Income Taxation,* Fisher and Fisher (1942, p. 94) write:

Such a tax policy would discourage mansions and encourage factories. When rich men are an offense in the eyes of the relatively poor, it is because of their big domestic establishments and their big spendings, not because of their big savings and big industrial plants. Snobbery goes with the idle and extravagant way of living—with diamonds and retinues of servants; but snobbery is seldom seen in a big factory where the owner himself works. In fact, few workers in democratic America object to the rich man who lives and works like a poor man—who puts his gains into instruments of production, not into instruments of consumption.

They conclude the chapter on social consequences this way:

Thus again we point out that the transcendent consideration must be the general effects of the tax system on the general welfare. So we come back, as always, to the most practical consideration of all: that it is good policy to harness up the saver as we would harness up a willing race horse and let him have his head, rewarding him with a little sugar instead of whipping him (which only makes him sulk)—all this on the theory that his race is our race and it is to our interest to promote his saving but restrict his spending. (p. 105)

Two distinguished economists from Cambridge University, writing two decades apart, each eloquently state the fairness case for a progressive consumption (expenditure) tax. Nicholas Kaldor, in his classic monograph, *An Expenditure Tax* (1955, p. 53) writes:

An Expenditure base would tax people according to the amount which they take out of the common pool, and not according to what they put into it. An inhabitant from Mars, admiring the highly intricate arrangements whereby men in society satisfy their needs in common through mutual cooperation, would surely be puzzled to discover that each individual's contribution to the finance of socially provided benefits depends not on the sum of benefits he receives from the community but on his personal contribution to the wealth of others. It is only by spending, not by earning or saving, that an individual imposes a burden on the rest of the community in attaining his own ends. In all his other activities his own interests and the interests of the community run not counter to one another but parallel....

The implication of this argument is that in considering what constitutes the fairest tax system we cannot stop short of reflection on the social consequences of individual behavior, and the effects on behavior of the tax system itself. Though questions of incentives are usually regarded as quite distinct from questions of equity, in the last analysis it is impossible to arrive at any ultimate criteria of "fairness" without taking the economic and social repercussions of individual behavior into account.

The second Cambridge economist, Nobel laureate James Meade, writes in his preface to the report by the Institute for Fiscal Studies, *The Structure and Reform of Direct Taxation* (1978, pp. xv–xvi):

There may be some degree of inevitable conflict between these two objectives of "efficiency" and "equality." But the clash can be minimised...and the structure of the tax system is one important element in the outcome.

An appropriate structure for this purpose...would be a basic reform of direct taxation which levied a charge on what people took out of the economic system in high levels of consumption rather than what they put into the system through their savings and enterprise.

The last ingredient is of the utmost importance. By shifting the tax base in this way all forms of enterprise—big or small, privately owned, state owned or labour-managed—would be able to plough back their own profits or to borrow the savings of others free of tax for all forms of economic development. But at the same time wealthy persons who were maintaining a high standard of living by dissaving from their capital wealth would be more heavily taxed than at present.

A possible political reaction to this would, I suppose, be for the "left" to reject it because it gave an opportunity for private capitalist enterprise (as well as for state enterprise and labour-managed enterprise) to invest more and to expand employment opportunities, and for the "right" to reject it because it would hit the rich who were living on inherited property. My hope is that the opposite would happen—that the "left" would welcome the egalitarian over-tones and the "right" the opening up of opportunities and incentives for all forms of enterprise. Indeed, if we are to find a reasonable base of political con-sensus in our mixed economy, I can see no better fiscal contribution to this end than a tax structure of this kind.

In an article in the *New Republic* (Feb. 28, 1976, p. 15), Martin Feldstein of Harvard (later Chairman of the Council of Economic Advisors in the Reagan administration) advocates a progressive con-sumption tax, commenting:

The idea that everyone's tax should depend on how much he consumes, regardless of how that consumption is financed, appeals strongly to our sense of fairness.

Lawrence Summers of Harvard (Deputy Secretary of the Treasury in the Clinton administration) also believes a consumption tax is fairer. In his article, "An Equity Case for Consumption Taxation," Summers writes (1984b, p. 258):

First, there is the question of choosing a fair base for taxation. Thomas Hobbes argued that there was greater justice in taxing people on what they took from the social pot (their consumption) rather than on what they contributed (as measured by their income). In many cases, this value judgment seems com-pelling. Should not some tax be paid by a wealthy man who draws down his wealth to maintain a high rate of consumption? It is not unreasonable for the profligate borrower, who lives beyond his income, to pay taxes on his pleasures?

Critics of the consumption tax point to the apparent counter-example of the miserly millionaire who enjoys great wealth but pays little tax. This argument has never seemed very compelling to me. If an individual forgoes consumption and allows his wealth to be used to contribute to productivity and growth, why should he be taxed? This question is hard to answer convincingly, since any proceeds earned and the interest on them will ultimately be taxed if they are spent.

I want to dwell on this argument for a moment because I think it is very important. A consumption tax is, in a very real sense, less coercive than an income tax. Under an income tax, persons who earn and save must pay tax. In the words of the old joke, "The reward of energy, enterprise, and thrift is taxes." Under a consumption tax, enterprise and thrift are unpenalized, and even energy and effort can escape taxation as long as their fruits are saved.

It is interesting to compare the principle of taxing according to withdrawal from the pie with the principle of taxing according to ability to pay. In most cases, the two principles yield a similar pattern of tax across households because high- consumption households generally possess high income, wealth, and hence high ability to pay. In some cases, however, the two principles yield very different taxes for particular households. It is here that the ability-to-pay principle deserves more careful scrutiny than it often receives.

Many analysts, and virtually all income tax advocates, take it for granted that ability to pay is the sole criterion by which to judge fairness. For example, in his article entitled "The Superiority of the Income Tax," Goode's (1980) entire discussion is limited to assessing which tax more accurately reflects ability to pay. Even Aaron and Galper (1985, pp. 20–21), who advocate a household tax with a saving deduction, make this ability-to-pay argument:

Fairness dictates that those with the same ability to pay should pay the same tax.... Consumption in our view is simply not an accurate measure of each person's ability to pay or of total economic capacity. Accumulations of wealth confer valuable economic and social benefits to their owners even if the wealth is not consumed. Accordingly, wealth accumulations should be incorporated into any measure of ability to pay. Unlike a consumption tax, a tax on income can reach accumulations of wealth that are not actually consumed during the accounting period. Thus we take income to be the proper object by which to measure ability to pay.

In his presidential address at the 1989 meeting of the American Economic Association, Pechman says (1990, pp. 6, 9):

Economists have long had trouble with the "ability to pay" concept. In recent years they have revived the old notion that consumption measures ability to pay better than income does. I believe that the person in the street is right and that we should continue to rely on the income tax to raise revenue in an equitable manner.... I conclude that income is a better indicator of ability to pay than consumption...

But on reflection, the ability to pay principle contains an element of expediency: tax a person more, simply because the person is able to pay more. But it seems reasonable to contend that a principle of fairness ought to consider what each person adds to and subtracts from the economic pie. It ought to consider how a person's economic behavior affects others. From this perspective, it seems fairer to tax a person according to what that person subtracts from, rather than adds to, the economic pie.

Progressive consumption tax advocates believe that fairness should take account of the consequences for others. True, a person may get satisfaction from saving as well as consuming. But saving benefits others by raising investment and hence future productivity. Consumption benefits only the person who consumes the resources.[8]

In chapter 2 we presented arguments for raising the U.S. saving rate. A higher saving rate will raise the real wage of all workers, including low-skilled workers; it will therefore reduce absolute poverty faster for low-skilled persons able and willing to work. A higher saving rate will preserve our future international standard-of-living ranking, and will contribute to the "ascent of man" through technological progress. True, the household that saves is not motivated by any of these consequences. But for a USA Tax advocate, these consequences are nevertheless relevant to fairness. Why should we tax S less than C? Both S and C are motivated by self-interest. But S's behavior leads to certain positive consequences for others while C's does not. So, yes, we deem it fair to tax S less than C.

In their monograph, Fisher and Fisher (1942, p. 101) address this issue by referring to a passage from John Stuart Mill. In a section entitled "Ability to Pay," they write:

It is said that the rich man who, in order to save, chooses to live like a poor man, can afford to pay more than the really poor man. John Stuart Mill answered this with characteristic incisiveness. He said:

"It has been further objected that, since the rich have the greatest means of saving, any privilege given to savings is an advantage bestowed on the rich at the expense of the poor. I answer that it is bestowed on them only in proportion as they divert their income from the supply of their own wants to a productive investment, through which, instead of being consumed by themselves, it is distributed in wages among the poor. If this be favoring the rich, I should like to have it pointed out what mode of assessing taxation can deserve the name of favoring the poor."

Feldstein (1976, p. 16) makes the same point when he writes:

A switch to a consumption tax is likely to increase the nation's rate of saving. With more saving available, our rate of investment would rise and our capital stock would grow larger. This increase in the amount of capital per worker would increase productivity and therefore raise real wage rates. Workers as a whole would therefore gain indirectly as well as directly from this tax reform.

The affluent often object that high income taxes inhibit their ability to save, thereby reducing national investment to the detriment of everyone. True enough. The progressive consumption tax puts each affluent household to the test. High-saving affluent households will indeed enjoy a tax cut, enhancing their ability to save more; in the extreme, the thrifty affluent will pay little tax. But low-saving affluent households will pay more tax.

Thus a progressive consumption tax creates a new covenant with the affluent. It says to them: If you save, thereby raising investment, productivity, and the wage of the average worker, you will be rewarded with a lower tax. But if you consume, subtracting resources from the economic pie for your own benefit, you will not be so rewarded. The aim is not to penalize consumption, but to reward saving that will lead to higher future output and consumption.

Income tax advocates worry about the concentration of wealth that might result from such a covenant with the affluent. For example, Pechman (1990, p. 9) writes:

Under an expenditure tax, taxpayers who save could accumulate large amounts of wealth over a lifetime. Many, but by no means all, expenditure tax advocates support wealth or estate and gift taxes to prevent excessive concentrations of wealth. But the history of transfer taxation in this country and abroad provides little assurance that effective death and gift taxes would be levied to supplement an expenditure tax.

Progressive consumption tax proponents plead guilty to the charge that their tax promotes wealth accumulation better than the income tax. The accumulation of wealth by households is matched by the accumulation of real capital (machinery, technology) that raises the productivity and real wage of the average worker. When persons accumulate, the corresponding real capital benefits others. When they stop accumulating and consume, they benefit only themselves. The progressive consumption tax strikes this bargain: accumulate and your tax will be low; decumulate and consume, and your tax will be high. Your tax will depend on how your behavior affects others.

In my view this new covenant with the affluent implies that gift and estate taxes should be terminated, with the revenue replaced by increasing the consumption tax rates that apply to the affluent. The aim would be to increase the incentive of the affluent to abstain from excessive consumption, leaving more resources for capital accumulation that benefits the average household in the future (McCaffery 1994a, 1994b, 1995).

From this perspective, this future benefit to the average household is more important than any harm that may result from some additional concentration of wealth in the hands of affluent thrifty households. Concern about vague political consequences of such concentration is a poor reason to use an income tax to reduce everyone's accumulation of wealth, thereby harming everyone's future standard of living. The reform of rules governing campaign financing and lobbying is a more direct approach to the political problem that avoids harmful economic side effects.

Consumption tax advocates differ over what should be done about estate and gift taxes. The 1995 USA Tax bill makes no change in these taxes. Those who advocate a consumption/gift/bequest (CGB) tax instead of a consumption tax clearly share the view of income tax advocates (like Pechman) that donors should be taxed on gifts and bequests. But anyone who believes that each person should be taxed according to what he actually withdraws from the economic pie should prefer a consumption tax to a CGB tax, and support the termination of estate and gift taxes because these transfers of wealth do not entail any actual consumption.

But don't many of the affluent take pleasure directly from earning and accumulating, not simply from consuming? Undoubtedly they do. But progressive consumption tax proponents are interested in the impact on others. You may enjoy earning and accumulating for its own sake, but this is not sufficient reason to tax you heavily. Only when you take a huge slice of the economic pie for your own enjoyment will you be heavily taxed—not because there is anything wrong with enjoying the slice, but because it leaves less for others.

Summers believes that this new covenant with the affluent will probably result in a more progressive household tax. Why? He explains (1984b, p. 260):

Further, under a consumption tax, saving decisions would no longer be distorted. This would surely mitigate one of our major barriers to increased progressivity under the income tax. Progressivity could no longer be opposed on the grounds that high marginal rates excessively interfere with saving decisions. Under a consumption tax, the higher marginal propensity of the rich to save would not constitute a justification for opposing progressivity. In economists' language, the optimal tax is likely to be more progressive if efficiency costs can be minimized.

In other words, when higher tax rates on the rich are proposed for the income tax, it is rightly objected that this will compel many who would have saved to pay tax instead. But under the consumption tax, this objection dissolves. An affluent household can escape high tax rates by saving. Hence Congress may well be willing to set a higher tax rate on the consumption of the rich than on the income of the rich. If so, the household consumption tax will turn out to be a more progressive tax than the household income tax.

So in conclusion, let us restate the fundamental fairness principle of the progressive personal consumption tax: Using progressive rates, tax each person, not according to his ability to pay, or according to his productive contribution, but according to what he withdraws for his own benefit and enjoyment, thereby leaving less for others to consume or businesses to invest.

Other Fairness Arguments for a Progressive Consumption Tax

There are several other fairness arguments given by proponents of a progressive consumption tax: (1) the income tax penalizes the saver, while the consumption tax does not; (2) important components of income cannot be taxed in practice; (3) consumption is often (though not always) a better measure of ability to pay than income; and (4) "winner-take-all" excesses would be mitigated by it.

To understand the first argument, consider two persons, C and S, who work in period 0 and retire in period 1. Assume they earn the same wage in period 0. C saves nothing in period 0, nobly facing starvation in period 1 in order to keep our example simple. S saves in period 0 and dissaves in period 1. They receive no inheritance and leave no bequest. Under the income tax they both pay the same tax on wage income in period 0; but because S chooses to save, S pays tax on capital income in period 1. Hence S pays more lifetime tax than C simply because S chooses to save in period 0 and C doesn't.

By contrast, a consumption tax is neutral between S and C. S pays less tax than C in period 0 thanks to the saving deduction, but pays more tax in period 1 when the saving is withdrawn and consumed. It turns out that S and C will pay the same present value of lifetime tax.[9] What happens if we change the example so that S consumes less than she accumulated, leaving a bequest at death? Clearly, S would pay less tax than if she had consumed more and left no bequest. Hence, if she leaves a bequest, S would pay less lifetime tax than C. In this case, the consumption tax would actually favor S over C.

Some analysts prefer a consumption/gift/bequest tax to a consumption tax. Under a CGB tax, S would be taxed on her bequest as well as her consumption. If this is done, then S will still pay the same lifetime tax as C. Aaron and Galper (1985, p. 67) emphasize that they support a consumption/gift/ bequest tax (which they call a cash flow income tax), not a consumption tax. They write:

Under the [cash flow income tax] the tax on income that is saved is deferred until the savings are consumed or transferred to others by gift or bequest. End-of-lifetime wealth, representing unexercised potential consumption of the taxpayer, is included in the tax base of the final tax return. The inclusion of most such transfers is essential to the cash flow income tax. If bequests and gifts were taxed as lightly under the cash flow tax as they are under the current estate and gift taxes, a cash flow base would measure only consumption instead of income.[10]

Mieszkowski (1980, p. 182) apparently also prefers a consumption/gift/bequest tax to a tax levied only on actual consumption:

Some equity arguments against a consumption-based system are easily countered. It is sometimes asserted, for example, that the ability of the miser to escape taxation by failing to consume proves the inequity of consumption taxation. Yet if the miser's estate is taxed as consumption at the time of his death, he—who consumed virtually nothing—and the person who consumes all his wage income as soon as it is received would pay the same tax calculated on a present value basis. The miser accumulated wealth at a very rapid rate and would pay a large tax at the time of death.

Advocates of a CGB tax emphasize this lifetime perspective and the lifetime neutrality of a CGB tax between persons S and C even if S leaves a bequest. This has led to an unfortunate confusion. Some income tax advocates apparently believe that the equity case for a consumption (expenditure) tax rests primarily on its alleged lifetime neutrality. For example, Pechman (1990, p. 8) says: "A basic difference between the income and expenditure taxes is in the time perspective of the two taxes.... Advocates of the expenditure tax regard the lifetime perspective as a major advantage."

But our basic equity argument for the consumption (not CGB) tax, explained in the preceding section, has nothing to do with a lifetime perspective or the alleged lifetime neutrality between S and C. Our argument is simply this: In each year, it is fairer to tax a person according to what he takes out of the pie for his own enjoyment, rather than what he contributes to the pie that year. It follows that S should pay less tax than C in any year that S actually consumes less than C. The lifetime perspective is irrelevant to our basic equity argument for a progressive annual consumption tax.

Thus anyone who accepts the argument of the preceding section believes it is indeed fair for S to pay less tax than C if S leaves a large bequest in the example above. Why? If S consumes little over her lifetime, leaving more resources for others to consume and businesses to invest, then she deserves to pay a low lifetime tax. It should also be pointed out that the incentive to work and save may be stronger if tax can be permanently escaped as long as one never actually consumes resources.

The second fairness argument for a consumption tax is that important components of income cannot be taxed in practice. Economists generally agree with Henry Simons, author of the classic monograph *Personal Income Taxation* (1938), that income equals consumption plus the change in net worth, whether the change is "realized" or not. Hence if the market value of a household's corporate stock rises from $2,000 to $3,000, this accrued capital gain constitutes $1,000 of income even if the stock is not sold. Because it is generally impractical to tax all accrued capital gains (and such gains may be a large percentage of income for some wealthy households but not others), the income tax is inevitably unfair: certain components of income are fully taxed while others are untaxed. Although capital gains are eventually taxed if and when the stock is sold, the delay in taxation (often many years) greatly reduces the effective rate of taxation. Moreover, inflation over the long period further compounds the mismeasurement.

This escape from taxation of accrued property income is emphasized by Kaldor (1955, p. 89), who writes:

The authors who argue in favour of taxing income rather than expenditure because it involves heavier taxation of property have got hold of precisely the wrong end of the stick. They take it for granted, without argument or analysis, that "income" from property is a simple and unambiguous concept, and that under a system of income taxation it is possible to lay hands on the true income accruing from work. In fact, as we have shown, this is not the case, and an income tax on the existing pattern involves serious differentiation in tax treatment in favour of property owners. An expenditure tax would remove that differentiation—it would ensure that a man who lives on a certain scale and obtains his income from work is not more severely treated than another man who secures the same standard of living from capital.

Bradford (1980, p. 85), who supervised the U.S. Treasury's *Blueprints,* similarly reviews the problems in measuring accruing income, and emphasizes the same point:

It is in dealing with problems of the sort described above that a consumption base has its most obvious administrative advantage. Under a consumption tax accruing wealth is wholly irrelevant. There is therefore no need to measure it, no need to estimate depreciation, accruing capital gains, or accruing rights in pension systems or life insurance policies. There is no need to measure the effect on shareholder wealth of retained earnings or of any other events at the corporate level. If no cash transaction takes place, there is no need to be concerned about those forms of wealth in calculating the base of a consumption tax. It is that simple.

This leads to the third fairness argument: consumption is often a better measure of ability to pay than income. Recall that our main argument for the consumption tax rejects ability to pay as the most important criterion of fairness. But even if one regards ability to pay as the most important criterion, there is a case for the consumption tax. Why? Because in practice, important components of genuine income, such as accrued capital gains, will be omitted from taxable income. Hence taxable income will in practice be an unsatisfactory measure of ability to pay. Will actual expenditure be better? Kaldor's (1955, p. 47) answer is yes:

The point is that no definition of Income, which is a plausible one for purposes of tax assessment, can measure taxable capacity. Accruals from the various sources cannot be reduced to a common unit of spending power on any objective criteria. But each individual performs this operation for himself when, in the light of all his present circumstances and future prospects, he decides on the scale of his personal living expenses. Thus a tax based on actual spending rates each individual's spending capacity according to the yardstick which he applies to himself. Once actual spending is taken as the criterion all the problems created by the non-comparability of work-incomes and property-incomes, of temporary and permanent sources of wealth, of genuine and fictitious capital gains resolve themselves; they are all brought into equivalence in the measure in which they support the actual standards of living.

There is an important demographic group for whom consumption is generally a much better measure of ability to pay than income: retirees.

Many retirees have accumulated significant wealth, and therefore have a significant ability to pay. Their income is low, but they use their wealth to finance consumption. Thus their consumption is generally a better measure of their ability to pay than their income.

Basing the household tax on consumption rather than income would facilitate fairer treatment of retirees under certain programs. For example, suppose that Medicare seeks to have each household pay a share of its medical bill that is scaled to its ability to pay (Seidman 1994b, 1995). To do this, Medicare would utilize information reported on the household's tax return. A household tax return that reports consumption will generally be more useful than a return that reports income in measuring the household's ability to pay.

The final argument, which concerns fairness and efficiency, is that winner-take-all excesses in our market economy would be mitigated by a progressive consumption tax. In their provocative book, *The Winner-Take-All Society*, Frank and Cook (1995, pp.viii, 212–214) write:

The reward structure common in entertainment and sports—where thousands compete for a handful of big prizes at the top—has now permeated many other sectors of the economy...we conclude that...much of the rivalry for society's top prizes is both costly and unproductive....

Because the ultimate purpose of earning income is to consume it, a progressive tax on consumption makes entry into winner-take-all tournaments less attractive for the same reasons that a progressive tax on income does. And by effectively reducing the prizes received by winners, a progressive consumption tax also reduces the incentives to engage in positional arms races.

Is a Consumption Tax Really a Wage (Labor Income) Tax?

One of the favorite charges of income tax advocates is that any consumption tax is really a wage tax, and a wage tax is obviously unfair. For example, Pechman writes (1990, pp. 8–9):

A tax that omits saving from the tax base can be shown to be the same as a tax applying only to labor income and exempting all property income. Several expenditure tax advocates have, in fact, proposed a tax on labor income on grounds of simplicity and administrative feasibility. Most people would be appalled by a proposal to substitute a wage tax for an income tax, yet that is essentially what expenditure tax proponents are advocating.

The charge has been repeated many times (see, for example, Warren 1975). Here's one rationale for the charge. There are two ways to encourage saving. The first is to deduct saving in the year it occurs, taxing only consumption. The second is to exempt the yield from saving (capital income) and tax only wage income. Because the two methods appear to give similar encouragement to saving, it seems natural to assert that the two taxes are really the same. It is also clever for the income tax advocate, because most citizens immediately judge a wage tax to be unfair, but have an open mind about the fairness of a graduated personal consumption tax.

To answer this charge, consumption tax advocates call to the stage a character whose notoriety surely matches the miser: the lazy heir (Seidman 1980, p. 12; 1990b, p. 50). The lazy heir inherits a large fortune, uses it to finance a high level of consumption, never works a day in his life, and dies leaving no bequest. Now what tax would the lazy heir owe under a wage tax? Zero. At the annual April 15 news conference at his plush estate, the lazy heir holds up his wage tax return—an empty sheet of paper. With servants surrounding him, he complains that it is most fortunate that he owes no tax, not having worked, because he needs every bit of his fortune to maintain his mansion. Needless to say, he is a favorite on the evening news.

Under a graduated personal consumption tax, however, the lazy heir would pay his share. His high consumption would incur a high tax. As he sells the stocks and bonds he inherited, his cash inflow would record the sale of assets. Because there is no corresponding saving deduction, his taxable consumption would correspond to his asset sales. In fact, a graduated personal consumption tax would tax the lazy heir more heavily than an income tax. Under an income tax, he would be taxed on capital income. But under a consumption tax, he would be taxed on the wealth he consumes each year.

Most citizens believe that people who enjoy high consumption should pay high tax. A graduated personal consumption tax assures this. A wage tax does not. Thus when it comes to fairness, a graduated consumption tax is surely not a wage tax.[11]

Breaking the Capital Gains Deadlock

Nowhere is the difference between a consumption tax and a wage tax more crucial than in the capital gains debate. The debate has deadlocked because it has been fought under the straightjacket of the income tax. Advocates of cutting the income tax rate on capital gains argue that it will promote saving and investment. It seems plausible that cutting the tax rate on any component of capital income—interest, dividends, or capital gains—will probably encourage more saving in the favored form.

But by proposing a capital gains cut within the framework of the income tax, advocates are implicitly arguing for moving the income tax toward a labor income (wage) tax. Let's take the argument to the limit. Suppose we cut the tax rate on interest, dividends, and capital gains to zero—we exempt capital income. Then we would indeed have converted the income tax to a labor income (wage) tax. The odds are high that there would be a significant boost to saving.

But opponents argue that a labor income tax would be unfair. Persons who do not work but finance high consumption with capital income and inherited wealth would owe no tax, while someone who works to finance normal consumption would pay a corresponding tax. Under an income tax framework, these opponents argue that fairness requires taxing all income at the same rate.

As an advocate of the comprehensive income tax, Pechman was elated by the 1986 Tax Reform Act. In his last major article before his death, Pechman (1990, p. 11) writes: "The Tax Reform Act of 1986, a major step toward comprehensive income taxation, greatly improved the fairness and efficiency of the tax system. The major accomplishments of the act are as follows.... For the first time since 1921, realized capital gains were made taxable as ordinary income. This is the keystone of comprehensive tax reform."

Pechman concedes that capital gains should be adjusted for inflation before being taxed. He recognizes that it could make matters worse to do this only for capital gains due to games that might be played between inflation-adjusted and unadjusted assets, so he makes this recommendation (Pechman 1990, pp. 12–13): "An inflation adjustment of asset prices should be incorporated in the tax law as part of the computation of real capital gains and losses, real interest income expense, and real inventory and depreciation allowances. The adjustment of interest is admittedly difficult, but the widespread use of computers should ease the administrative and compliance problems."

Although the Treasury recommended inflation adjustments for most components of capital income in its 1984 tax reform proposal, inflation adjustment was not incorporated into the 1986 Act, partly due to its complexity. Despite this omission, Pechman (p. 13) gives this warning:

"Restoration of a tax differential between capital gains and ordinary income should be resisted at all costs.... Aside from the correction for inflation, the one additional reform needed in the capital gains tax is to include in the tax base unrealized capital gains transferred by gift or at death. Taxing such gains would reduce the lock-in effect of the tax on transfers of assets and eliminate a source of horizontal inequity."

Yet in 1990 Congress raised the top bracket rate from 28% to 31%, but kept the maximum tax rate applying to capital gains at 28%; and in 1993 raised the top bracket rate to 39.6%, but held the maximum capital gains rate at 28%. So a wide differential has again opened up.

Consumption tax advocates argue that as long as the debate is straightjacketed by the income tax, it is likely to deadlock. Each side is dug into its trenches. Proponents of the rate cut emphasize saving and investment. Opponents emphasize the unfairness of permitting affluent people to enjoy high consumption but pay low tax when it is financed by capital gains.

But conversion to a progressive consumption tax would break this deadlock. Under a progressive consumption tax, income from whatever source is never taxed per se. It is only taxed, and always taxed, if it is consumed, and at graduated rates. The capital gains controversy would be terminated in the stroke that cuts the Gordian knot: conversion of the personal tax base from income to consumption.

Does a Personal Consumption Tax Burden the Young and the Old?

Pechman (1987, p. 272) writes: "Most people would be puzzled by a tax that imposes the heaviest burdens on families precisely when they consume the most (the young and the old) and the lightest burdens on those who are able to save (the middle-aged)." The recommended practical options in chapter 4 address Pechman's charges. Here we briefly note how. Under the USA Tax, the young will not have to pay the whole tax on "big-ticket" items (house, car) in the year of purchase—the tax will be spread over time if the item is loan financed. We will see that this spreading is feasible under the USA Tax, but not under a sales tax, VAT, or flat tax. Today's elderly will be protected from double taxation by a transition rule exempting a percentage of "old" wealth accumulated after paying income tax. Future elderly will pay more tax because they will pay less tax during middle age due to the saving deduction.

Conclusions

No matter how important it is to raise national saving and investment, it is unacceptable to do it by adopting an unfair tax. According to USA Tax proponents, unfairness is indeed the downfall of several consumption taxes that would promote saving and investment—the sales tax, the VAT, and the flat tax. But they believe a strong case can be made that there is a consumption tax that is fair: the USA Tax that has as its main component a household consumption tax with graduated rates and top-to-bottom progressivity. Of course, even if one believes the income tax is slightly fairer that the USA Tax, one might still support conversion to the USA Tax because of its likely impact on saving and investment. But USA Tax advocates do not believe there is a trade-off. To them, it is fairer to tax each household according to how much it subtracts from the economic pie for its own enjoyment—its consumption—than to tax it according to how much it adds to the pie through its productive effort.

4   Practical Options

The household component of the USA Tax takes as its ideal the personal consumption tax, while the business component takes as its ideal the subtraction value-added tax (VAT). This chapter discusses the practical options involved in the design of each component of the USA Tax.

It must be emphasized that the best way to handle various practical options continues to evolve as USA Tax designers set out tentative solutions and receive feedback. For example, there are important differences between Senator Domenici's 1994 article and the March 10, 1995, detailed Explanation in *Tax Notes* authored by Christian and Schutzer (hereafter referred to as "the 1995 Explanation"), and the bill of April 1995 (hereafter referred to as "the 1995 bill"). As further feedback accumulates, there will surely be further changes. Therefore this chapter will not regard the solutions offered in 1994 or 1995 as necessarily permanent. It will draw on these tentative decisions as well as on the contributions of tax specialists who have analyzed these practical options.

The Household Tax Return

The household tax takes as its ideal the personal consumption tax. How should a household compute its consumption this year? Surely, not by trying to keep and add hundreds of receipts for each consumption expenditure. Instead, the strategy is indirect and practical: Sum this year's cash inflows, and then subtract this year's nonconsumption cash outflows. There are only a small number of inflows to add and nonconsumption outflows to subtract, in sharp contrast to the hundreds of consumption expenditures.

This indirect, practical cash flow method of computing household consumption is the contribution of Irving Fisher of Yale University and his brother Herbert Fisher in their path-breaking monograph *Constructive Income Taxation*. The Fishers write (1942, pp. 4–5):

It is strange that those who recognize that "spendings" are the only fair and logical base for taxable income often fail to realize how practical and simple is its application. How do we figure what we spend in a day? We need only two data:

1. The amount we had to spend; that is, what we had or received during the day.

2. The amount we did not spend; that is, the amount left over as determined by counting at the end of the day.

The application of this simple procedure to the tax problem is the only novelty of the present proposal.

Moreover, the data needed for this calculation are considerably more trustworthy than those used in our present income taxes, which often depend on debatable estimates.

We propose, then, to reckon the taxable spendings, not by adding together the separate items spent for food, clothing, rent, amusements, etc., but by adding together the gross receipts from all sources and then deducting all items of outgo other than "spendings."

The U.S. Treasury's *Blueprints for Basic Tax Reform* (1984, pp. 101–102) explains the strategy this way:

This chapter presents a proposal for a consumption base tax as an alternative to a comprehensive income tax. Called the Cash Flow Tax because of the simple accounting system used, this system is designed to replace the current taxes on the income of households, individuals, trusts, and corporations.

The central feature...is the use of cash flow accounting for financial transactions to obtain a measure of annual consumption for any individual or household. The principle involved is very simple. A household could use monetary receipts in a year for three purposes: personal consumption, saving, and gifts. By including all monetary receipts in the tax base, including the proceeds of sales of assets and gifts received, and allowing deductions for purchases of assets and gifts given, the annual consumption of a household could be measured without directly monitoring the purchases of goods and services.

The tax return under a personal consumption tax instructs the household to compute this year's consumption. An example of a personal consumption tax return is given in table 4.1. The items on this return will be explained in this chapter. It should be emphasized that the actual USA household tax return, when finalized, may differ from this tax return in certain respects.

Table 4.1
A personal consumption tax return

	Cash inflows	
1.	Wages and salaries	60,000
2.	Interest, dividends, cash withdrawals from business	3,000
3.	Withdrawals from savings accounts or investment funds	2,000
4.	Sale of stocks and bonds	2,000
5.	Loans (excluding consumer durable loans)	2,000
6.	Cash gifts and bequests received	1,000
7.	Pension, Social Security, and insurance cash benefits	0
8.	Total (add lines 1,2,3,4,5,6,7)	70,000
	Nonconsumption cash outflows	
9.	Deposits into savings accounts or investment funds	9,000
10.	Purchase of stocks and bonds	7,000
11.	Loan repayments (excluding consumer durable loans)	1,000
12.	Cash charitable contributions and gifts given	1,000
13.	Higher education tuition (investment component)	2,000
14.	Total (add lines 9,10,11,12,13)	20,000
15.	Consumption (subtract line 14 from line 8)	50,000
	Deductions	
16.	Personal exemptions	10,000
17.	Family allowance	7,000
18.	Old wealth deduction	3,000
19.	Total (add lines 16,17,18)	20,000
20.	Taxable consumption (subtract line 19 from line 15)	30,000
21.	Tax	10,000
22.	Payroll tax credit	4,000
23.	Net tax (subtract line 22 from line 21)	6,000

Cash Inflows, Not Incomes

Although compromises may in certain instances be necessary, it is important to keep the consumption tax ideal clearly in mind. The aim of the household tax return is to instruct the household to compute its consumption during that calendar year by the addition and subtraction of specified items. The items to be included are those required to yield an accurate computation of consumption.

Household consumption is generally financed by cash—currency or check—perhaps with a short lag after the use of a credit card. To compute its consumption, the household must add up all cash inflows. It then subtracts nonconsumption cash outflows. What's left is consumption. This technique of computing this year's consumption by adding and subtracting this year's cash flows is crucial to the practical implementation of a personal consumption tax. For this reason, the tax is sometimes called a cash flow consumption tax.

Thus the key question is not whether an item is "income," but whether it is a cash inflow that must be included in order to yield an accurate computation of consumption. Similarly, the issue is not whether a particular cash inflow item is "taxable." What is taxable is consumption. The term "cash inflow" should replace "income" on the household tax return, and in any description of the USA Tax. The terminology should convey the fact that the USA Tax is a cash flow consumption tax, not an income tax.

The Nondeductibility of Taxes Withheld or Paid

At first glance, it might seem that taxes withheld or paid during the calendar year are nonconsumption cash outflows that should be deducted in computing the tax base. But a good case can be made that it is better to make all taxes (federal, state, and local) nondeductible. This is the approach taken in the 1995 bill and the 1995 Explanation. The tax base then becomes private consumption plus taxes (withheld or paid).

There are at least three arguments for this treatment of taxes. First, taxes are often consumption outflows—they often finance the consumption of public services. For example, suppose persons A and B have the same income and saving, but A lives in a community with high taxes and high public services, while B lives in a community with low taxes and low public services. A has higher public consumption than B, lower private consumption than B, and the same total consumption as B. It seems fairest for A and B to pay the same personal consumption tax. This is achieved by making local taxes nondeductible.

Second, the choice among taxes and user fees by state and local governments will not be distorted. To avoid distortion, either all taxes and user fees must be deductible, or all, nondeductible. But it is impractical to make indirect taxes—sales or excise taxes—deductible because the household never writes a check for an indirect tax. Thus the only way to avoid distortion is to make all taxes and fees nondeductible.

Third, when a state or local government spends $X, its citizens will bear a tax cost of $X because there will be no partial offset due to a deduction of $X on the USA Tax return. The removal of this offset should induce a more optimal weighing of the benefits and costs of state and local government spending.

In their exposition and advocacy of a personal expenditure tax, Courant and Gramlich (1984, p. 33) recommend eliminating the deductibility of state and local taxes:

These taxes are now treated in a rather confused way by the federal income tax; standardizing the treatment would improve the income tax and make it more like an expenditure tax. State and local user fees, the most efficient tax assessed by subnational governments, are already nondeductible on federal returns. Other state and local taxes are deductible on federal returns but only for those who claim itemized deductions—a minority of taxpayers, most of whom have relatively high incomes.

The proper tax treatment, under either an income or expenditure tax, is to consider all state and local taxes as payments for public consumption expenditures, and to eliminate their deductibility.

The consequence of making the USA Tax payment nondeductible should be noted. Suppose a household's cash inflows sum to $100,000, its nonconsumption cash outflow is $0, USA tax withheld is $20,000, and consumption (plus other taxes) is $80,000. With no deduction for USA tax withheld and a 20% tax rate, USA tax owed would be $20,000. Alternatively, if the $20,000 withheld were deductible but the tax rate were 25%, then USA tax owed would again be $20,000. The 20% is called the "tax-inclusive" rate because it is applied to the $100,000, while the 25% is called the "tax-exclusive" rate because it is applied to the $80,000. Adopting the rule that all taxes are nondeductible implies using the tax-inclusive rate.[1]

Nonconsumption Cash Outflows

To compute household consumption, all nonconsumption cash outflows must be subtracted. The issue is not whether a cash outflow is "saving," but whether it is "nonconsumption." Thus business expenses (such as genuine home office expenses) should be deductible. Similarly, the purchase of real estate (other than a home the household will occupy and land it will live on) should be deductible, just as the sale of such real estate should be included in cash inflows.[2] Thus the 1995 bill strays from a consumption tax when it denies a deduction for the purchase of such real estate. The 1995 Explanation (pp. 1573–1575) argues at length that real estate is not a "savings asset." But that is not the key issue. As long as the household is not purchasing consumption, the cash outflow should be deductible.

Note that fluctuation in the market value of the household's portfolio is irrelevant. The aim is to compute the household's consumption, and the strategy is to follow the cash: add all cash inflows, then subtract all nonconsumption cash outflows. Cash withdrawals from saving accounts or investment funds are included in cash inflows, and cash deposits are included in nonconsumption cash outflows. Any fluctuation in the market value of the household's portfolio is irrelevant to the computation of the household's consumption.

Interest and Dividends

If $1,000 of interest or dividends is actually paid in cash (check) to a household, the $1,000 is included in line 2 on the personal consumption tax return. If the household then deposits the $1,000 in a savings account or investment fund, this $1,000 deposit would be included in line 9.

But suppose the $1,000 of interest or dividends is generated in a savings account or investment fund and is simply retained by the account or fund. Then the $1,000 is not included in line 2 or line 9. Of course, it would be possible to pretend the household had actually received $1,000 in cash and then deposited it immediately in the fund; then $1,000 would be included in line 2 and there would be a cancelling $1,000 deposit in line 9. But there is no need for this pretense. The aim of this tax return is not to compute interest, dividends, or income, but to compute consumption. Only cash inflows actually received by the household need to be recorded on the personal consumption tax return.

Sale of Financial Assets

If revenue from the sale of corporate stock X is $10,000, then $10,000 is added to cash inflows on line 4. If the $10,000 is used to buy other stock Y, then there is a corresponding deduction of $10,000 on line 10. If it is used to finance consumption, then there is no cancelling deduction, and the $10,000 is appropriately taxed.

What must be emphasized is that $10,000 is not the contribution of stock X to this year's income. For example, if the market value of X was $9,000 on January 1, and if the stock was sold for $10,000 on December

31, then stock X's contribution to this year's income is $1,000—its rise in value. But $10,000 is included in cash inflows on line 4 because the aim is not to measure this year's income, but to compute this year's consumption. Thus sale of stocks and bonds replaces capital gains on the household tax return.

Borrowing to Buy Financial Assets

Borrowing is clearly a cash inflow that may potentially finance either expenditure on real goods and services or the purchase of a financial asset. To accurately compute this year's consumption, borrowing must generally be included in cash inflows; an important exception is explained in the following section on consumer durables. Thus loans (excluding consumer durable loans) appear on line 5. Correspondingly, loan repayments (principal plus interest) should then be deductible. Hence repayments (excluding consumer durable loan repayments) appear on line 11.

Consider what can happen if borrowing is excluded (and loan repayments are not deductible). If a household borrows $20,000 to buy corporate stock, its actual consumption is unchanged, but its computed consumption would fall $20,000 if the loan is excluded from line 5, because it would deduct $20,000 for the stock purchase on line 10. This year it would pay too little tax. True, in future years it would pay too much tax because repayments would be nondeductible and computed consumption would therefore exceed actual consumption. But with graduated tax rates, things may not "even out" (the present value of taxes may well diverge from the correct amount). Things will definitely not even out if the loan is not fully repaid.

But even if things "evened out," there is no persuasive reason why these errors in computing annual consumption should be permitted. The errors can be avoided simply by including loans in line 5 and deducting repayments on line 11. A loan and its repayment entails a definite cash transaction between the household and a lending institution. These cash transactions can be audited and verified as definitely as other items on the tax return such as wages and salaries. Hence these cash transactions should be used to compute annual consumption accurately.

It must be emphasized that the issue is not whether borrowing is "income." It isn't. The issue is whether its inclusion in cash inflows is required to accurately compute the household's consumption. Similarly, repayment of a loan—principal plus interest—is a cash outflow not used for consumption; it should therefore be deductible. Again, there is an important exception that will be explained later in the section on consumer durables.

Because some taxpayers initially will be puzzled if loans are included on the household tax return, it may be tempting to try to get by without it. The 1995 version of the USA Tax bill succumbs to this temptation by excluding all borrowing from cash inflows. The 1995 Explanation declares that borrowing is not gross income and that the USA Tax should restrict cash inflows to gross income. But as explained previously, this decision in itself would cause computed consumption to be less than actual consumption. A special complex method is then devised to try to prevent this. "Non-exempt borrowing" is a key item on the complex Schedule S (Net Savings Deduction Calculation) shown in the 1995 Explanation—perhaps the most complex part of the 1995 bill.

However understandable, this convoluted approach is a serious mistake and should be reversed. The simple correct solution of including borrowing and deducting repayments has been recommended by virtually all commentators on the personal consumption tax.

In their illustrative tax return, Fisher and Fisher (1942, p. 8) include under cash inflows "any borrowing less repayments," and note (p. 10) that "No other income tax system includes in the reckoning the principal of loans."

Similarly, Kaldor (1955, p. 192) includes "money borrowed" in his cash inflows. *Blueprints* (U.S. Treasury 1984, p. 111) states:

Normally, under cash flow accounting, receipts from a loan would be handled through qualified accounts. An individual would be required to report the loan proceeds in his tax base in the initial year. (Of course, if he used the loan proceeds to purchase investment assets through a qualified account in the same tax year, there would be no net tax consequences.) Subsequent interest and principal payments would then be deductible from the tax base in the following years.

In contrast to most other commentators, *Blueprints* does allow the taxpayer the option of excluding borrowing and repayments. But Graetz (1980, p. 183) explains the pitfalls of this option for financial assets:

Thus cash flow treatment of investment assets and loans would tend to be more equitable and efficient than exemption of yield and should be adopted as the general rule.

Including loans in receipts would be a significant departure from the current income tax treatment and would undoubtedly require considerable taxpayer education before adoption, but the offsetting deduction for investments purchased with loan proceeds should ease the transition. Cash flow reporting of loans does not seem likely to cause new administrative problems, although potential under-reporting of loans must be considered.

In his *Harvard Law Review* article, Andrews (1974, p. 1153) writes:

Business and investment loans would be treated, just like ordinary investments, on a simple cash flow basis. Loan proceeds would be reported as income in the year received, and repayments of interest and principal would be deductible when paid. This treatment is unfamiliar, but would represent a clear net simplification for reasons similar to those favoring a cash flow accounting for ordinary investments...

Inclusion of loan proceeds in income would not ordinarily require large tax payments in the year of a loan, because normally such loans are to pay for capital investment that would be immediately deductible under a consumption-type tax. Cash flow accounting for loans and capital investments would assure, however, that deductions based on capital investment are limited to one's own net cash investment.

In November 1984, the U.S. Treasury issued *Tax Reform for Fairness, Simplicity, and Economic Growth.* The report became known as Treasury I. In a section on the personal consumption tax (called "consumed income tax" in the report), it states (p. 192):

The principle of taxing consumption determines the treatment of loans under a consumed income tax. Since repayment of debt is equivalent to saving, a deduction would be granted for such repayment and for payments of interest; similarly, the proceeds of borrowing would be included in taxable consumption. If net loan proceeds were not included in the tax base, taxpayers could "game" the tax system simply by borrowing funds, depositing them in a qualified account, and taking a deduction for the increase in their "saving." Purchasing assets with borrowed funds does not add to net saving, and therefore would not qualify for a deduction under a consumed income tax. Although the present value of the taxes might not be affected, since the taxpayer could not deduct the repayments and interest on the loan, omitting borrowing from the base would enable the taxpayer to postpone the liability. This would disrupt the timing of government receipts and would seem unfair.

If all borrowing is excluded, the USA Tax will rightly be criticized by tax experts. In response to the 1995 Explanation, Warren presents some examples showing the problems that result from excluding borrowing to finance the purchase of financial assets. He concludes (1995, p. 1108):

Rather than adopting cash flow taxation of personal consumption, the USA tax proposes a net savings deduction for individuals, which is called the Unlimited Savings Allowance. The foregoing analysis suggests the following tentative conclusions regarding this proposal.

1. It would be much simpler to implement the standard cash flow taxation of personal consumption.

2. Adoption of the net savings deduction instead of including borrowed amounts in the tax base permits deferral of the tax beyond the date of consumption.

I recommend that USA Tax designers heed the advice of these experts on the personal consumption tax and generally include loans in cash inflows (except for consumer durables, as explained next) and include loan repayments (except for consumer durables) in nonconsumption cash outflows.

Consumer Durables

The person who buys a television for $1,000 does not consume $1,000 in the year of purchase. In theory, a household's consumption this year of any durable is the rent it would have paid had it rented rather than owned. If everyone rented durables, there would be no practical problem. If a person paid a $200 annual television rental, $200 would be automatically taxed because the $200 rental expenditure would not be deductible. The problem, of course, is that there are no actual rental payments.

The simplest practical option is "prepayment": tax the whole purchase in the year it occurs. This is achieved simply by not permitting a deduction for any expenditure on a durable. True, too much tax is paid in the purchase year. But too little (zero) is paid in all subsequent years. It evens out. As *Blueprints* (U.S. Treasury 1984, p. 109) states:

To assure that the entire consumption value is included in the tax base, the appropriate treatment of consumer durables is to allow no deduction on purchase.... In other words, purchase of a consumer durable would be treated the same way as current consumption of goods and services. The reason for this approach is that the price paid for a consumer durable should reflect the present value of future services the buyer expects to receive. Including the value of durable goods in the tax base at the time of purchase produces, in effect, a prepayment of the tax on the value of future consumption services.

It should be noted that a household's expenses for maintenance, repair, or improvement of any durable should be nondeductible because these costs would be reflected in the rent charged if the household rented rather than owned. Hence these expenses should be regarded as a cash outflow for consumption.

Although prepayment is acceptable for most durables, it would be better if the tax could be spread over time, just as the flow of consumption is spread over time. As several commentators (cited later) have noted, this is easily done if the household borrows to finance the purchase. To achieve tax spreading, these commentators recommend that while expenditure on the durable should remain nondeductible, the taxpayer should exclude borrowing for the durable from cash inflows (in contrast to other borrowing, which must be included in cash inflows on line 5). These commentators then recommend, naturally, that the loan repayments (principal plus interest) should not be deductible so the household would be implicitly taxed on each repayment (in contrast to other loan repayments that would be deductible on line 11). For this reason, consumer durable loans are excluded from line 5 of the tax return, and consumer durable loan repayments are excluded from line 11.

This treatment postpones the consumer durable tax on the amount equal to the loan. It therefore improves the accuracy of the computation of each year's flow of consumption, appropriately eases the tax in the year of purchase, and spreads it over time as the loan is repaid. Because it improves the accuracy of measuring the household's annual consumption, I recommend that this treatment be required, not optional.

For example, suppose a car is purchased for $25,000 with the help of a $20,000 auto loan. Even though the $25,000 expenditure is nondeductible, exclusion of the $20,000 loan means that only $5,000 ends up being taxed in the year of purchase. If the repayment period is five years and the interest rate is 7%, then the household would exclude $20,000 from cash inflows in the year of purchase when the loan is obtained, but the annual loan repayment (principal plus interest) of $4,559 would be nondeductible and hence implicitly taxed each year.[3]

It is desirable to spread the tax of a durable over time because consumption from the durable is spread over time. By contrast, it is undesirable to defer taxation of nondurable consumption. Only loans for specific durables should be excluded; loans for nondurables should be included because, to the maximum extent practical, tax should be paid in the year when consumption occurs.

I agree with other commentators that, for practical reasons, the implicit short-term borrowing that occurs with credit card purchases

should be ignored and "repayments" should therefore be nondeductible. Consider a household that runs up a $2,000 bill on its credit
card in December 1996 and pays it with a $2,000 check in January 1997.
Strictly speaking, it has implicitly borrowed $2,000 from the credit card
company in December and consumed $2,000 in December. If this were a
normal explicit loan, it would have to include $2,000 as a cash inflow in
1996 and pay tax on it in 1996; the repayment in January 1997 would be
deductible so it would of course pay no tax in 1997. Analysts recommend ignoring implicit credit card borrowing, however, so the household would pay tax in January 1997 when it makes its nondeductible
"repayment" of the implicit loan.

It must be recognized that the use of a loan determines its proper
treatment in a computation that tries to measure this year's consumption. Recall that a loan to finance the purchase of a financial asset (i.e.,
stocks or bonds) should be included in cash inflows and repayments
should be deducted as a nonconsumption cash outflow. But a loan to
finance a specific consumer durable should be excluded from cash
inflows and repayments should be nondeductible in order to spread the
tax over time just as the consumption is spread over time. And a loan to
finance nondurable consumption should be included in cash inflows,
and repayments should be deductible because tax, like consumption,
should occur in the year of purchase.

To implement these distinctions, the household must include any
loan in cash inflows (on line 5 of the tax return) unless the loan secures a
specific consumer durable and is used to purchase that durable. Under
an audit, if a nonreported loan is detected, the household must verify
the consumer durable secured and purchased by the loan. Similarly, if
the household deducts a loan repayment (on line 11 of the tax return), it
must be prepared to verify that the loan was in fact included in cash
inflows on a previous tax return because it financed the purchase of a
financial asset or nondurable consumption.

There are two further complications concerning consumer durables.
First, maintenance expenses and property taxes should be nondeductible because these expenses would have been reflected in the rental
price if the durable had been rented rather than owned. Second, if the
durable is resold, then resale revenue should be excluded to avoid double taxation because tax has already been paid on the whole value of the
durable—whether it was prepaid in the year of purchase, or paid
through the implicit taxing of loan repayments. In theory, a household

should be indifferent between renting and owning if the present value of the rental payments equals the purchase price plus the present value of maintenance expenses and property taxes minus the present value of the expected resale price; so potential owners will bid the purchase price up or down until this equality holds. It follows that to make an owner pay the correct present value of taxes—the amount a renter pays—the purchase price, maintenance expenses, and property taxes should be nondeductible and the resale revenue should be excluded from cash inflows.

For example, suppose after five years the television purchased for $1,000 is sold for $300. Because the tax has been fully paid on $1,000 worth of television, but the person has only used $700, it would be double taxation to tax the person on the $300 of resale revenue. The person has paid too much tax on the television. Hence resale revenue should normally be excluded from cash inflows because the person is entitled to another $300 of tax-free consumption. In effect, the exclusion of the $300 rebates the tax on the $300 because it was not consumed.

Similarly, suppose the person trades in the television for $300, thereby reducing the price of a new television by $300 (say from $1,500 to $1,200). By ignoring the implicit revenue from the trade-in we get the right result: $1,200 of consumption will be taxed. The person will eventually consume $1,500 of the new television, and receives in effect a rebate of tax on the $300 that was not consumed.

As *Blueprints* (U.S. Treasury 1984, p. 109) states: "To assure that the entire consumption value is included in the tax base, the appropriate treatment of consumer durables is to allow no deduction on purchase and to exclude sales receipts." A problem arises if the durable is sold for a higher price than its purchase price. As several analysts have suggested, here it seems reasonable to require the capital gain to be included in cash inflows because it might be claimed that the person has only been taxed on consumption equal to the purchase price (the "cost basis"). In effect, only sales revenue up to the purchase price is excluded from cash inflows; revenue in excess of the purchase price (the capital gain) is included in cash inflows and taxed. The 1995 bill follows the current income tax law by proposing to tax any capital gain on the sale of a durable.

This treatment of consumer durables can be applied to owner-occupied housing (Seidman and Lewis 1996a). If a household buys a home for $165,000, the expenditure would be nondeductible. But if it obtains a loan (mortgage) of $150,000 with a repayment period of thirty years and an interest rate of 7%, then the household would exclude $150,000 in the year of purchase when the mortgage is obtained, but the annual loan repayment (principal plus interest) of $11,297 would be nondeductible and hence implicitly taxed. Tax would be prepaid on the $15,000 not financed by the mortgage. Expenses for maintenance, repair, and improvement should all be nondeductible because these costs would be reflected in the rent if the household rented rather than owned. For the same reason, property taxes should be nondeductible. Note that when a major home renovation is financed by a loan, the tax would be spread over time because the loan would be excluded and repayments would be nondeductible.

It is important to consider a particular feature of housing: the resale price is often comparable to the purchase price. This implies that the home owner pays too much tax prior to resale even with mortgage spreading, and the exclusion of resale revenue is necessary to refund this excess tax. It would be better if the homeowner paid less tax prior to resale, and received a smaller refund at resale.

A very rough way to do this is to make a portion of the mortgage payment deductible, but to tax the nominal capital gain when the house is sold and the seller becomes a renter. The partial mortgage payment deduction prevents the overpayment of tax prior to resale, and the taxation of the nominal capital gain in an economy with inflation reduces the tax refund. We therefore have a very rough justification for retention of a deduction for mortgage interest payments provided the nominal capital gain is taxed when the owner sells the home and becomes a renter. To tax the nominal capital gain, all maintenance and improvement expenses should be nondeductible, but the basis of the home should be adjusted as under current income tax law in order to compute the capital gain upon sale. Tax should be postponed if the seller buys another residence, but the current exclusion of $125,000 of capital gain should be terminated so that the capital gain is fully taxed. The 1995 bill prescribes this treatment.

It is worth citing several commentators who support various aspects of this treatment of consumer durables and loans secured by and used to purchase the durables. Graetz (1980, p. 197) writes:

I recommend an identical approach for the taxation of consumer durables and the taxation of housing.

• No deductions should be permitted for the purchase of consumer durables and housing; yield in the form of imputed rents should be ignored; and when the sale price does not exceed the original cost, no amount need be included in the expenditure tax base upon sale. When the sale price of a house or consumer durable exceeds original cost, such excess should be added to expenditure tax receipts, when received.

• Loans for the purchase of consumption goods or housing should ordinarily not be included in expenditure tax receipts, and no deduction should be allowed for interest or principal payments. A dollar limitation might be used in implementing this rule.

• No deductions should be allowed for property taxes on consumer durables or owner-occupied homes.

Mieszkowski (1980, p. 190) writes in a section on consumer durables:

Consumer loans do not significantly complicate the picture. They can be treated in one of two equivalent ways.... One way of dealing with consumer loans is to include loan proceeds in receipts at the time the loan is made, and then to allow a deduction for interest and amortization of the loan as it comes due. Alternatively and equivalently, the proceeds of the loan and subsequent interest and amortization can all be disregarded.

If the second approach is applied to the purchase of a house, the consumption tax paid will approximate a tax imposed on annual services derived if the service life of the house corresponds to the life of the mortgage. When a $50,000 house is purchased and is fully mortgaged, and if loan proceeds are excluded, with mortgage interest and amortization not deductible, a consumption tax will effectively be paid on interest and mortgage amortization.

I support Mieszkowski's recommendation except that I would require his second approach (loan exclusion and repayment nondeductibility) in order to assure that tax, like consumption, is spread over time.

Andrews (1974, pp. 1154–1155) writes:

But it is much simpler and quite acceptable just to leave ordinary consumer loans and credit arrangements out of account. The effect of that is to treat payments on account of consumer loans, rather than the use of the loan proceeds, as taxable consumption expenditures.... In cases of loans to finance purchase of consumer durables, this treatment would generally correspond more closely to real consumption than would inclusion of the loan proceeds immediately in income.

Note that I would restrict the exclusion to loans that are secured by and used to purchase a specific consumer durable because only durables justify a technique for spreading tax over time.

To summarize my recommendation: (1) all "nonsecured" loans (loans not secured by and used to purchase a specific consumer durable) should be included in cash inflows; "secured" loans (loans secured by and used to purchase a specific consumer durable) should be excluded; (2) all "nonsecured" loan repayments (principal plus interest) should be deductible; "secured" loan repayments should be nondeductible. If a household excludes a loan, it must be prepared to verify that the loan was secured by and used to purchase a specific durable. If the household claims a deduction for a loan repayment, it should affirm that the loan was not secured by a consumer durable. These rules apply whether the loan and durable purchase occurred before or after USA Tax enactment.

The 1995 bill makes expenditure on durables nondeductible. It excludes all loans for any purpose. It makes all loan repayments nondeductible with one important exception: home mortgage interest payments. It should be noted that the 1995 bill does terminate the deductibility of property taxes and home equity loan interest payments. The bill also terminates the $125,000 capital gain exclusion, so that when a homeowner sells and becomes a renter, the capital gain will be fully taxed.

Thus I agree with the 1995 bill's treatment of any consumer durable financed by a loan secured by the specific durable. By contrast, however, I would restrict the loan exclusion to such consumer durable loans.

Finally, note that under a sales tax, VAT, or flat tax, the burden of purchasing a consumer durable cannot be spread over time; it must be fully borne in the year of purchase. Of all consumption taxes, only the personal consumption tax permits such spreading through its cash flow treatment of loans and repayments.

Gifts, Bequests, and Charitable Contributions

It is important to remember that a problem arises only from gifts and bequests made "externally" to another independent household (charitable contributions are external by definition). Gifts or bequests to a spouse or to children living in the same household would have no tax consequences because they are "internal."[4] Initially, assume the gift or bequest is in cash. Then other forms will be considered: corporate stocks, consumer durables, and consumer nondurables.

Under a personal consumption tax, a household should be taxed according to the resources it actually withdraws from the economic pie for its own consumption; it should not be taxed on the resources it leaves in the pie for other households to consume or for businesses to invest. A donor household does not consume resources when it gives a cash gift, bequest, or charitable contribution. Hence the gift, bequest, or contribution should be tax deductible, just like saving—it is a noncon-sumption cash outflow. If the donee (recipient) household saves it, the donee should not be taxed. When and if the donee consumes it, it should be taxed.

As Graetz (1980, p. 201) writes: "An expenditure [consumption] tax is intended to impose a progressive levy on consumption, and the donee, not the donor, will spend the amount of the gift or bequest. The com-mentators tend to agree, therefore, that an expenditure tax should exclude gifts and bequests from the donor's tax base and include such amounts in the donee's receipts."

Domenici (1994, pp. 302–303) adopts the same position:

Is making a bequest rightly considered consumption? For reasons of fairness and efficiency, we conclude that it is not. A bequest is not consumption because it is not an exchange for goods or services. In fact, it is almost the opposite of consumption. Inheritance is merely a change of ownership and not a taxable event; the consumption comes when that inheritance is spent by the heir for goods and services...

By treating inheritance as regular income to the recipient not consumed by the donor, the Nunn-Domenici plan maintains all its incentives for saving. Donors do not pay taxes on money they never spend. Thus, they will have no additional incentive to consume their savings before they die and, therefore, will be more likely to make capital available to others. Recipients are treated similarly; they face the standard decision of either consuming and paying tax or saving and avoiding tax.

I agree. I would go further and recommend that estate and gift taxes be terminated because these transfers of wealth do not entail any actual consumption (McCaffery 1994a, 1994b, 1995). The revenue lost should be replaced by raising the consumption tax rates that apply to the afflu-ent. From this perspective, a donation should not be taxed under any tax because the donation is not actual consumption.[5]

By contrast, under a personal consumption/gift/bequest (CGB) tax, the donor should be taxed on the cash gift and bequest (and perhaps also the charitable contribution). A CGB tax advocate believes that two persons with the same ability to consume should be taxed equally, regardless of how much each actually consumes.[6]

As Domenici argues, the consumption tax advocate believes it is fair-er to tax a person only on what he actually withdraws from the eco-nomic pie for his own enjoyment, and that it is better to give him an incentive to preserve the wealth he has accumulated rather than consume it. It should also be emphasized that the incentive to work and save may be stronger if tax can be permanently escaped as long as one never consumes the earnings.

A consumption tax is clearly simpler to implement than a consumption/gift/bequest tax. The CGB tax will encounter complexities similar to those faced by the estate and gift tax. Aaron and Galper (1985), who advocate a CGB tax (which they call a cash flow income tax), devote several pages to the practical details of treating gifts, bequests, and trusts. For example, they write (pp. 96–97):

Bequests pose the same problems encountered under the current estate tax: how to value assets for which no market price is readily available and how to arrange deferred payment schedules when the estate is illiquid. Current law contains workable but overly generous procedures for dealing with these problems. They need to be retained but tightened. As noted earlier, averaging arrangements should be available for bequests that would otherwise push the taxpayer into higher tax brackets.

The most serious problems would arise from techniques currently used to avoid estate and gift taxes that could be carried over to the cash flow tax system...

Opportunities to avoid tax with these devices and others like them would have to be severely curbed under the cash flow income tax. In some cases, a change of law would be easy to enforce, in others, extremely difficult...

These practical difficulties and all estate tax planning efforts would disappear by choosing a consumption tax instead of a CGB tax and by terminating estate and gift taxes.

Under both a consumption tax and a CGB tax, cash inheritances must be included by the donee (the recipient). Note an interesting consequence. Suppose a donor gives $10,000 to a donee who consumes it. Under the consumption tax, only the donee is taxed on the $10,000. Under the CGB tax, the donor is taxed on the $10,000 gift, and the donee is also taxed on the $10,000 of consumption.

Now consider gifts of corporate stock (or bonds) under a consumption tax. Suppose the donor gives stock to a donee who retains it this year. Recall that the strategy in computing a household's consumption—whether a donor's or a donee's—is to follow the cash, because consumption is generally financed by cash. The transfer of stock is neither a cash inflow for the donee nor a nonconsumption cash outflow for the donor. Hence there should be no tax consequence this year for donor or donee under a personal consumption tax. If and when the heir later sells the stock for $10,000 and consumes $10,000, the heir will pay tax on the $10,000 of consumption. Note that if the donor bought the stock after enactment of the personal consumption tax, she has already received a saving deduction for it.[7]

Next, consider a gift of a consumer durable. Suppose the donor gives a used car (bought several years ago) to a son or daughter as a college graduation present. The donor has already fully prepaid the tax. Ideally, the donor should get a tax rebate, and the donee should have to pay tax equal to that rebate. But how much should the rebate be? There is no actual cash transaction to provide a clear-cut answer. If the car is new and financed by borrowing, then there would be further complications. Finally, consider a piano bought many years ago. How would it be valued? On practical grounds, we recommend denying the donor a deduction (a rebate of tax) and permitting the donee to ignore any durable received as a gift. Thus for practical reasons the ideal would be sacrificed: the donor would continue to bear the full tax on the durable despite the fact that he has given it to the donee, who would consume it without paying tax.

This treatment of durables would encourage donors to give gifts of cash rather than newly purchased durables, because the donor will generally be in a higher tax bracket than the donee. Thus parents will be encouraged to give cash to their college graduate for the purpose of buying a car, rather than buying the car and then giving it to the graduate. If so, the donee who receives the cash will pay the tax due to its inclusion on line 6 of the donee's tax return; the donor will not pay tax due to its inclusion in nonconsumption cash outflows, line 12.

Although some commentators regard the resulting reduction in tax as a problem, I disagree. The aim should be to tax each household according to its consumption at graduated rates. If the college graduate is now one household, and the parents another household, then each should apply the tax rate schedule to its own consumption. In fact it is the college graduate, not the parents, who consumes the car. The appropriate tax is therefore the one that applies to the graduate's household. Note that a high school student living with her parents does not have her own household, so there is no "external" gift when she receives cash for a car or the car itself.

Of course, it would simpler to ignore all gifts and bequests, including cash. A donor would get no deduction for giving cash. A donee would ignore the receipt of any cash gifts or bequests when adding cash inflows. This is the current income tax treatment for gifts and bequests. It is also the treatment in the 1995 USA Tax bill. But simply ignoring gifts and bequests risks seriously understating the consumption of wealthy heirs, thereby undermining the fairness of the tax. This exclusion would permit an heir to obtain a huge saving deduction upon receiving a large inheritance.

To summarize, a sensible compromise is to conform to the consumption ideal for cash gifts (donor deducts, donee includes), but not for consumer durable gifts (donor does not deduct, donee does not include). The transfer of stocks and bonds would not in itself directly affect either the donor or donee's tax.

Finally, consider charitable contributions. Two objectives must be distinguished: accurately computing the donor's consumption and providing an incentive to make such contributions. To accurately compute the donor's consumption, the treatment should be the same as in the case of a gift to another independent household. A cash contribution should be deductible on line 12 because it is a nonconsumption cash outflow—the donor does not withdraw resources for his own enjoyment through this use of cash. A gift of stocks or bonds should not be deductible because it is not a nonconsumption cash outflow.[8] And for the practical reasons discussed earlier, the value of a gift of consumer durables (or other goods) should not be deductible. The 1995 bill contains a deduction for charitable contributions.

But there is also the objective of providing an incentive. With all saving deductible under the personal consumption tax, a deduction for charitable contributions may not induce as much giving as it does under a personal income tax. If an additional incentive is judged desirable, it would be possible to provide a tax credit for charitable contributions. The tax credit would be independent of the computation of the household's consumption and the tax based on that consumption—hence it would be in addition to the deduction required to accurately compute the household's consumption. The 1995 bill does not contain a tax credit for charitable contributions.

State and Local Government Bond Interest

It is indisputable that state and local bond interest is a cash inflow that must be added to other cash inflows to accurately compute the household's consumption. Excluding such bond interest from the computation would cause a serious error in computed consumption for some affluent households. The correct treatment is therefore obvious: include state and local bond interest in cash inflows. Note once again that the issue under a personal consumption tax is not whether to tax a particular component of income. It is simply whether inclusion is necessary for an accurate computation of the household's consumption. Thus I will use the term "exclusion"—exclusion from the computation of consumption—rather than "exemption" when referring to the personal consumption tax.

In the face of the obvious, three political forces will no doubt attempt to exclude bond interest from the computation: state and local governments, firms that market securities to the public, and holders of these bonds. State and local governments will claim they need and deserve federal assistance, and exclusion is a nice way to provide it; it will let them borrow at a lower interest rate. Firms that market securities like to impress potential clients with tricks to avoid tax, such as buying excluded bonds. Finally, current holders of state and local bonds naturally oppose inclusion.

Unfortunately, exclusion would damage the fairness of the USA Tax. It undermines the promise to make any household with high consumption pay a high tax. If only a few households took advantage, the harm would be tolerable. But the fact is that many of the most affluent households will hold these bonds.

So another way must be found to assist state and local governments (if such assistance is warranted). It is easily done. Let the federal government reimburse these governments for a percentage of their interest costs. For example, if including state and local bond interest causes yields to rise from 4% to 5%, let the federal government reimburse these governments 20% of their interest costs. Of course, some may doubt that any assistance is warranted. But if it is warranted, let the assistance be given this way so it does not undermine the fairness of the personal consumption tax.

Exemption does as much harm to the income tax as exclusion would do to the consumption tax. An eloquent attack on exemption is given in the classic monograph *Personal Income Taxation* by Henry Simons (1938, pp. 170–173) of the University of Chicago in a chapter devoted entirely to this exemption:

Any exemption of receipts by kind is clearly incompatible with the essential rationale of income taxes.... Most flagrant and least pardonable of all such errors of omission, however, is the exemption of the interest...of governmental bodies....for any government which does this is violating its responsibility for levying personal taxes equitably...

The exemption of the interest payments on an enormous amount of government bonds...is a flaw of major importance. It opens the way to deliberate avoidance on a grand scale; and it provides a method of avoidance which must give rise to serious inequities and to some diseconomies.... It is not easily accessible to persons, active in the control and management of enterprises, whose investments cannot be diversified without loss of the desired control over their firms. Indeed, this device of avoidance is entirely attractive only to the idle, passive holders of highly conservative investments. Thus the exemption not only undermines the program of progressive personal taxation but also introduces a large measure of differentiation in favor of those whose role in our economy is merely that of rentiers.

A recent Supreme Court decision seems to have clarified the constitutionality of including bond interest. In his recent text, *State and Local Public Finance*, Fisher (1996, p. 246) writes:

The federal tax exemption of state-local bond interest dates from the first federal Income Tax Act of 1913. For many years it was argued by some that the federal government did not have the constitutional authority to impose a tax on the income from state and local government securities.... [But] in a 1988 decision (South Carolina v. Baker), the Supreme Court ruled that the federal government does have the authority to tax state-local bond interest.

Economists are virtually unanimous in their condemnation of the tax exemption for state and local bond interest. Here is a sample. Fisher (1996, pp. 255, 262) writes:

If the objective of the tax exemption for interest on state-local government bonds is to subsidize government borrowing costs, then the tax exemption can be shown to be an inefficient subsidy in the sense that the federal government loses more than $1 of tax revenue for each $1 of interest cost saved by state-local governments...

Because of the problems created by the tax exemption of interest from state-local bonds, economists have long suggested that state-local governments issue taxable bonds with the federal government using a direct subsidy if it wished to reduce state-local borrowing costs. For instance, if a subnational government issued taxable bonds at an 8-percent rate when tax-exempt bonds had been yielding 6 percent, a federal subsidy equal to 25 percent of the state or local government's interest cost would reduce borrowing costs equally to the tax exemption. The prime advantage of this method is that it would cost the federal government $1 for each $1 saved by the subnational governments rather than more than $1, as is the case with the tax exemption. In other words, this direct payment would be a more efficient way for the federal government to subsidize state-local borrowing costs.

In their public finance text, Musgrave and Musgrave (1989, p. 562) write:

Federal tax policy gives general support to state and local borrowing by excluding interest on such securities from taxable income under the federal income tax...

But this particular form of aid is subject to criticism on two grounds. First, it interferes with the equity of the income tax structure. High-income recipients who receive tax-exempt interest pay less tax than do others with equal income from other sources. Moreover, the value of tax exemption rises with bracket rates so that vertical equity is interfered with. On these grounds alone, it would be preferable to provide such assistance as is desired in a way which does not involve tax preferences.

In his public finance text, Rosen (1995, pp. 365–366) writes:

The interest earned by individuals on bonds issued by states and localities is not subject to federal tax. From the [Haig-Simons income tax ideal], this exclusion makes no sense—interest from these bonds represents no less an addition to potential consumption than any other form of income. The exclusion originally followed from the view that it would be unconstitutional for one level of government to levy taxes on the securities issued by another level of government. However, many constitutional experts now believe such taxation would be permissible...

In sum, there is absolutely no objective case for exemption under the income tax or exclusion under the personal consumption tax. The damage to the fairness of the household tax—whether on income or consumption—cannot be overstated. It undermines the claim that anyone with high income, or high consumption, pays a high tax. It should be terminated to preserve the fairness of the household tax.

Should current bond-holders be given some kind of protection? Graetz (1980, p. 264) argues they should not, because it would be unfair to single out this group in a mixed economy where market and legislative changes are continuously imposing unexpected losses and gains. He writes:

Would not those who fervently argue for compensation (or other protection, perhaps through a grandfathered effective date) for losses suffered because of a change in law be appalled if similar protection were proposed for those who invested in Edsel or hula hoop production? But what is the difference between market and political processes that justifies such protection against political change? Such a justification becomes particularly difficult in a mixed economy, where the market is so often affected by political decisions.

Although Graetz's argument has force, advocates of the USA Tax face the political problem of securing enough support to achieve enactment.

It is therefore prudent to offer some protection. But it should not be done by distorting the computation of the household's consumption. Hence bond interest must be fully included on line 2 of the tax return to compute consumption accurately. Instead, some protection can be offered through the "old wealth deduction" (line 18), which will be described shortly.

Unfortunately, the 1995 USA Tax bill simply excludes state and local bond interest. No reason is given in the 1995 Explanation. But having excluded bond interest, the designers of the 1995 bill then try to prevent taxpayers from using excluded interest to obtain positive saving deductions, only permitting them to use excluded interest to reduce dissaving. To do this, they make excluded bond interest a key item of perhaps the most complex part of the 1995 bill: Schedule S (The Net Savings Deduction Calculation) shown in the 1995 Explanation.

Although the political judgment of the designers of the 1995 bill deserves respect, it is my view that they have underestimated the political cost of exclusion. There are two sources of political cost. First, the 1995 bill is forced to add a complex provision that tries to prevent households from using the exclusion to obtain positive saving deductions. Critics of the USA Tax rightly emphasize the complexity.

But second, and most important, exclusion undermines the political strength that comes with fairness. Advocates assert that the USA Tax is fair because it makes any household enjoying high consumption pay a high tax. But exclusion means that households that finance high consumption from excluded bond interest will pay little or no tax. It is hard to overemphasize the political damage this does to a proposal that seeks to be a fundamental tax reform.

Tuition for Higher Education and Vocational Training

Economic research supports the view that investment in human capital (education and training) raises a nation's economic productivity. It therefore makes little sense to allow a deduction for investment in physical capital but no deduction for investment in human capital.

One important difference between the USA Tax and the flat tax is that the USA Tax gives each household a higher education deduction while the flat tax does not. The flat tax provides an investment deduction for business, but no saving or investment deduction for households; this helps keep the flat tax household tax return no larger than a postcard. Although some deductible business expenditures constitute an investment in human capital, an important share of all human capital expenditures are made by households. So a household deduction is desirable.

College tuition expenditure has two components. The first is an investment that yields future taxable cash inflow when the former student earns higher compensation. This component should be treated like an investment in stocks and bonds: the expenditure should be deductible. Under this treatment, note that if $5,000 were borrowed to finance this component, the $5,000 would be included in cash inflows but there would be a cancelling deduction for a $5,000 human capital investment, so no tax would be owed.

The second component is consumption as the education occurs—the current enjoyment of all aspects of college life—and this should be treated like any consumption: the expenditure should be nondeductible. Room and board is also nondeductible consumption. College consumption financed by borrowing, like other nondurable consumption financed by borrowing, would be taxed in the year it occurs; borrowing would be included in cash inflows but there would be no cancelling deduction.

Of course, there is no unambiguous measure of the percentage of the total cost of undergraduate education that each component constitutes. But it would be possible to estimate percentages for the average undergraduate and apply them to all undergraduates. For example, suppose the estimated percentages are 50% investment, 50% consumption. Then for any student, 50% of undergraduate tuition might be made deductible. Students in vocational, technical, and graduate schools are primarily investing rather than consuming. It can therefore be argued that a higher percentage should be deductible for these students.

It is sometimes claimed that a dispute over percentages can be avoided if tuition is simply declared nondeductible. But this claim is incorrect. Nondeductibility means a choice of 0% investment and 100% consumption, which is even more disputable because it is so clearly incorrect. It is better to make the best possible estimate of the investment percentage, and allow this percentage to be deductible.

The 1995 bill provides a tuition expenditure deduction of $2,000 per person up to a maximum of $8,000 per household. Although this is an admirable step in the right direction, it does not go far enough; $2,000 is much less than the investment component of the typical college tuition.

A conservative estimate of the investment component might justify a deduction equal to 50% of tuition up to a maximum deduction of $5,000 in 1996.[9]

Pensions, Social Security, Insurance, and Medical Care

To compute the household's consumption accurately, the following cash benefits must be fully included in cash inflows: pension, Social Security, unemployment insurance, and life insurance. These appear on line 7 of the personal consumption tax return. If these benefits are saved, there is a corresponding nonconsumption cash outflow. With a progressive tax schedule, including these benefits will result in little or no tax for low-consumption recipients. The 1995 USA bill includes 85% of Social Security benefits. Under the current income tax, a portion of Social Security benefits are included for affluent retirees. If it is politically necessary to give nonaffluent retirees some temporary relief concerning Social Security benefits, it should be done through the "old wealth deduction" (line 18) discussed shortly, rather than by distorting the accurate computation of the household's consumption.

The 1995 bill excludes employer contributions to pensions from household cash inflows. This is equivalent to, but simpler than, including employer contributions in household cash inflows but permitting an equal deduction for saving. In contrast to the current income tax, employer contributions to life and health insurance are included in household cash inflows. They are treated as if the employer paid cash to the employee, who then used the cash to buy insurance. There is, however, an important difference in the treatment of life and health insurance under the 1995 bill.

Both employer and employee purchases of life insurance are treated like saving: the purchase is deductible, but benefits from the life insurance are included in the recipient's cash inflows. If the recipient initially saves the benefits, there would be an equal deduction so the recipient initially pays no tax. The recipient would only pay tax as she uses the benefits for consumption. Note that while averaging is necessary for a large lump-sum payment under an income tax, it is unnecessary under a consumption tax.

By contrast, employer and employee purchases of health insurance are not deductible so that these expenditures are treated as consumption. In turn, payments by health insurers—private companies or government—to medical providers on behalf of the household are excluded. This treatment is both practical and equitable. It avoids taxing as consumption a large hospital or doctor bill paid by the insurer.

The 1995 bill taxes all out-of-pocket medical payments because they are not saving. But the proper criterion is whether such payments constitute consumption. On the one hand, resources are withdrawn for private use. On the other hand, consumption of medical care seems different from consumption of recreation. For most goods and services, it is impractical to try to distinguish between expenditures to "avoid disutility" and expenditures to achieve "positive utility." But perhaps in the case of extraordinary medical expenses it is worth doing so. The current income tax permits a deduction for extraordinary out-of-pocket medical payments above a designated percentage of adjusted gross income. In my view, a similar deduction for extraordinary medical expenses should be retained under the USA Tax.[10]

Business-Financed Consumption

Although households generally finance most or all of their consumption, business firms finance some consumption for some employees or clients. Firms buy some employees cars, recreation, or vacations. They buy dinner or entertainment for some clients. Clearly, the integrity and fairness of the USA Tax requires that all consumption be taxed, however financed.

Two approaches are possible: first, attribute the expenditure to a particular individual for inclusion on the USA household tax return, so the individual is taxed on the expenditure; or second, deny the business firm a deduction for the expenditure on the USA business tax return, so the firm pays tax on the expenditure.

Under attribution, business-financed consumption would be attributed to the individual who actually consumes. If a firm spends $X on consumption for person A, then A would be required to add $X to cash inflows on his tax return. The advantage of this approach is that the tax appropriate for person A is applied to the $X.

There are problems with attribution. It may not be easy to attribute accurately and fairly. A firm may spend $Y to finance consumption jointly for its employees or clients. Although it would be simple to assume that each employee or client consumes an equal share, it may be inaccurate and unfair. For example, a recreational facility that employees can use without charge may be used repeatedly by one employee and never by another. Also, in contrast to self-financed consumption, employees and clients may have little choice about business-financed consumption. An employee or client may protest that she herself would never have made these expenditures.

The alternative is to deny the business firm a deduction for the expenditure on the USA business tax return. Ordinarily, the firm can deduct purchases from other firms. But a purchase that finances employee or client consumption would be nondeductible unless it is attributed to particular individuals who would then pay tax on the household tax return.

The 1995 bill generally follows this approach: attribution to individuals when feasible, otherwise, nondeductibility by the business firm.

"Old" Wealth

It cannot be overemphasized that the treatment of "old" wealth must be kept as simple as possible. Critics of conversion have quite properly attacked several complex treatments that have been proposed, especially the treatment included in the 1995 bill. The aim here must be to keep the treatment relatively simple while achieving a satisfactory degree of fairness.

Conversion from the income tax to any consumption tax—sales tax, VAT, flat tax, or USA Tax—creates a double taxation problem. People who accumulate wealth after paying income tax look forward to consuming that wealth without paying a second tax. Suddenly conversion occurs with the laudable objective of promoting saving. But people are often right to object: "It's unfair to tax me when I consume my 'old' (previously acquired) wealth. You are taxing me twice."

The double tax problem is a transitional problem. If people live their whole lives under an income tax, they are taxed on their labor compensation and capital income, but when they consume their accumulated wealth, there is no consumption tax. If people live their whole lives under a consumption tax, their saving is tax deductible, but when they consume their accumulated wealth, then they are taxed. In each case, there is one tax. But if people are caught in a conversion from the income tax to the consumption tax, then they must pay twice.

It is sometimes mistakenly thought that only the USA Tax has a double taxation problem. On the contrary, all consumption taxes do. The

USA Tax is the only consumption tax that tries to handle it. Advocates of the sales tax, VAT, and flat tax generally ignore the problem. Yet imagine the person who plans to consume old wealth suddenly standing at the cash register facing prices that are 20% higher due to a sales tax, VAT, or flat tax. Obviously, it doesn't matter whether the second tax is levied at the cash register or on April 15—it is still double taxation. Yet only the USA Tax has included provisions to reduce the problem.

Fortunately, the problem is not as bad as it seems. An important share of each household's old wealth hasn't even been taxed once yet, but would be taxed if the income tax were retained. A large share of pension funds accumulate without any income tax. The employer's contribution is untaxed and the interest earned is untaxed. If the income tax were retained, often the first tax would occur when pension benefits are paid. So taxing most withdrawals from pension funds under the consumption tax is exactly what would have happened under the income tax; it is not double taxation at all. Pension fund wealth is an important fraction of the financial wealth of many households.

Then consider people caught at conversion with an impressive set of consumer durables. If the durables were financed largely by loans, then this source of financing was not taxed under the income tax— loans are not taxable income. So taxing the loan repayments by making them nondeductible under the consumption tax would tax this consumption once, not twice. Recall the rule for loan repayments: they are deductible only if the loan has been included in cash inflows on a previous tax return. Since pre-enactment loans were not included, they are nondeductible.

If the durables were bought without borrowing, the source of financing was generally taxed under the income tax. But the flow of consumption services will remain tax-free; it is simply impractical to tax these flows for most durables under either an income or consumption tax. So these durables will also escape double taxation. Thus no matter how "old" durable wealth was financed, it will generally escape double taxation.

Next consider people who bought corporate stock years ago at prices that seem low by today's standards. True, the stock was generally bought after paying income tax. But as the stock appreciated in value each year, tax on the accrued capital gain was deferred. So when stock bought a decade ago for $2,000 is sold today for $10,000, only $2,000 of it has been previously taxed, and $8,000 would be taxed under the income tax. So taxing $8,000 under the consumption tax would be exactly what would have occurred under the income tax.

Finally, it should be recognized that an important fraction of wealth, especially wealth held by the rich, will not be consumed, but will be given away as gifts or bequests. Under a consumption tax (in contrast to a consumption/gift/bequest tax), the donor household will not be taxed again on this wealth. So "gift and bequest wealth" is already protected against double taxation.

Thus the double taxation problem is not as bad as it seems. Nevertheless, the problem still warrants treatment for wealth that has been accumulated from after-tax income, would not be taxed again under the income tax, but will in fact be consumed and hence taxed under the consumption tax unless there is an old wealth deduction.

In contrast to the 1995 bill, which includes a complex method for protecting all wealth holdings, I recommend a simpler method that protects wealth only up to a moderate ceiling. I seek to avoid the two extremes: no protection, which is simple but unfair; and complete protection, which is fair but excessively complex.

I do not recommend a deduction for old wealth above a moderate ceiling for three reasons. First, an important share of wealth above the ceiling will not be consumed, but will be given away as gifts and bequests, so it will not be taxed under the personal consumption tax; hence it is already protected, and a deduction would offer unjustified double protection. Second, large wealth holdings often include assets that are difficult to value. Third, there is a need to limit the revenue loss from the old wealth deduction.

Recall Graetz's argument (1980, p. 264) against giving protection to current holders of state and local bonds. He contends that tax conversion need not offer protection because people are not protected against many other unexpected economic and political changes. Nevertheless, there are two reasons for giving some protection. First, it is probably politically necessary to achieve enactment of the USA Tax. Second and more fundamentally, as Domenici (1994, p. 300) emphasizes, Graetz's "hardline" approach would be "both unfair and inconsistent with the overall policy objectives of the new tax system. Because this approach would penalize people who saved and invested, behavior the new system is designed to encourage, I categorically reject this approach."

Domenici does not go to the other extreme of seeking perfect fairness. Instead, he suggests a simple "amortization" schedule for deducting old wealth that would provide some protection (1994, pp. 301–302):

On the date of enactment all taxpayers would determine their total financial assets or old savings acquired before [the USA Tax]. This one-time calculation would...result in a relatively short and fixed transition period. The new system would allow each taxpayer an additional deduction—called a "previously acquired financial asset adjustment deduction"—for each of several years following the enactment of the new system. For example, the taxpayer could be entitled to a deduction equal to twenty percent of his or her total previously acquired financial assets for each of the five years following the date of enactment. This would provide full accommodation of old savings. However, revenue constraints may not allow Congress to go that far. Alternatively, the system could allow a deduction of ten percent for each of the three years following the date of enactment to achieve a partial adjustment.

In my view, this amortization method is the best solution to the old wealth problem provided it is limited to moderate wealth holdings (Seidman and Lewis 1996b). The complexity occurs just once: the computation of old wealth in the year of enactment. Thereafter, the household is taxed on its consumption (computed by cash flows) except that it can deduct a percentage of its old wealth, computed in the year of enactment, until it uses up its deduction (this is done on line 18 of table 4.1). Moreover, the complexity is reduced if there is a ceiling so that only moderate wealth holdings can be deducted, because large wealth holdings sometimes contain assets that are difficult to value.

For this one-time computation of deductible old wealth, the key question should be this: How much would the household have actually consumed, tax-free, under the income tax? For example, if a household has $50,000 in a bank account, and corporate stock that was purchased for $50,000, then it could have consumed $100,000 tax-free under the income tax.[11] But if the typical $100,000 household cumulatively consumes only $60,000, leaving the rest as a bequest, then the old wealth deduction schedule should assign it a cumulative old wealth deduction of $60,000.

Thus each household should be instructed to make a one-time computation of old wealth it held on December 31 before tax conversion, and submit its list of assets and computation with its first-year tax return. It should initially compute its maximum possible tax-free consumption under the income tax by adding its assets—bank accounts, purchase price ("basis") of stocks, and so on (note that most or all of its pension fund would be excluded because it would have been taxed upon withdrawal under the income tax). Next it should subtract its debt to obtain its potential maximum tax-free consumption under the income tax. But it would not actually consume this entire amount. So the household should be instructed to apply a schedule to this amount: for example, 80% of the first $50,000, 40% of the next $50,000, and 0% thereafter; the sum of these would be the cumulative old wealth it can deduct over several years. Note that with this schedule, the maximum deductible old wealth would be $60,000.

The household would then take an annual deduction each year until it exhausts its cumulative old wealth deduction. If the amortization period is five years, then the household would be instructed to deduct 20% of its deductible cumulative old wealth each year for five years. Note that with this schedule, almost all households would have positive taxable consumption for two reasons. First, the maximum possible annual deduction for any household is $12,000. Second, low-consumption households would generally be entitled to an annual deduction much smaller than $12,000.[12] Thus all households would exhaust their old wealth deduction in five years.

Note the key features of this amortization method. Once old wealth is computed, the annual deduction is simple and automatic: 20% of deductible old wealth for each of five years. There are no behavioral games to play. As soon as tax conversion occurs, each household can see clearly from its new tax return that it will be taxed according to its consumption, except that there are three deductions: personal exemptions, a family allowance, and a predetermined old wealth deduction.

By contrast, Aaron and Galper (1985) propose tracking each asset until it is sold in a future year. In the year of sale, the basis (cost) of each old asset would be deductible. Note that the sale might occur many years after the new system is in effect. I will call their prescription the "asset sale method." Aaron and Galper (pp. 78–79) admit: "The transition would take many years to complete; but once all assets acquired before adoption of the cash flow income tax had been sold or transferred to others by gift or bequest, taxpayers would generally not need to maintain any tax records of asset purchase prices."

An advantage of the Aaron-Galper asset sale method is that it uses only actual transactions—a deduction occurs only when the asset is sold. Nevertheless, Domenici (1994, p. 301) does not recommend their method for the following reason:

The main problem with the basis adjustment approach is recordkeeping. Proponents of this approach argue that this burden is no greater than the burden under current provisions that require individuals to keep track of their tax basis. However, the basis adjustment approach would require separating assets into those acquired prior to the new system's effective date and those acquired afterward. It would require keeping track of those assets until they are sold, thereby prolonging the transition period indefinitely.

Thus while the Domenici amortization method gets the complexity over with in the one-time computation of deductible old wealth, the Aaron-Galper asset sale method continues the complexity over many years. Another problem with the Aaron-Galper method is that taxpayers may be encouraged to manipulate when they choose to sell assets. Aaron and Galper try to guard against such manipulations by adjusting the basis for each year that the sale of the asset is delayed. But this adds complexity.

The 1995 bill follows Domenici's 1994 recommendation for taxpayers with old financial wealth less than $50,000 (excluding retirement accounts). Unfortunately, it prescribes a much more complicated method for taxpayers with old wealth greater than $50,000. First, these taxpayers must keep track of the "basis" (cost) of each asset sold in each subsequent year, as in the Aaron-Galper asset sale method. Second, these taxpayers must include the basis of stocks sold that year on a Schedule S (Net Savings Deduction Calculation) that also involves borrowing and tax-exempt bond interest—perhaps the most complex part of the 1995 bill, as we will see in the next section. Through Schedule S, the 1995 bill tries to prevent the use of the old wealth deduction from increasing positive saving, while permitting the deduction to reduce negative saving.

Kaplow, of Harvard Law School, demonstrates the perverse incentives created by this Schedule S treatment of old wealth (1995, p. 1112). He writes:

The theme that emerges is that the basis recovery system of the USA Tax is designed to reward immediate consumption over saving [f.n. I say "designed" without meaning to attribute intent. Perhaps the consequences were not fully appreciated]...The USA Tax forces taxpayers to consume their savings rather than keep them invested if they wish to benefit from basis recovery. Put another way, the USA Tax is relatively more generous to dis-savers in comparison to savers or individuals who maintain their prior savings intact.

But Kaplow hastens to add that "these problems can be largely remedied in a straightforward manner" (p. 1118). He notes that the kind of amortization schedule suggested by Domenici would avoid creating a perverse incentive to consume old wealth rather than preserve it:

An alternative that provided basis deductions that were independent of savings decisions, as by the use of an amortization schedule, would result in all taxpayers from the outset facing the marginal treatment associated with a pure, fully implemented consumption tax. Moreover, such a schedule could be as generous or stingy toward basis recovery as desired... (p. 1117)

I therefore recommend Domenici's 1994 amortization method, limited to moderate wealth holdings.

Finally, if it is politically necessary to give some temporary relief concerning interest on state and local bonds, or Social Security benefits, it should be done through the old wealth deduction rather than by distorting the accurate computation of the household's consumption. Thus interest on state and local bonds and Social Security benefits should be fully included in cash inflows (line 2 of the tax return for bond interest, line 7 for Social Security benefits) so that the household's consumption is accurately computed. But if the amortization period for the old wealth deduction is five years, a household that acquired state and local bonds at least a year before tax conversion might be permitted to increase its old wealth deduction by 80% of bond interest in year 1, 60% in year 2, 40% in year 3, 20% in year 4, and 0% thereafter. Similarly, a household that receives a Social Security benefit that was exempt from tax the previous year under the income tax might be permitted to increase its old wealth deduction by 80% of its benefit in year 1, 60% in year 2, 40% in year 3, 20% in year 4, and 0% thereafter (high-income retirees who are taxed under the current income tax would be ineligible for transitional relief). This approach assures that these transitional measures will be terminated by the end of the amortization period for deductible old wealth.

Eliminate Schedule S (the Net Savings Deduction Calculation)

Perhaps the most complex aspect of the 1995 bill and the 1995 Explanation (pp. 1520–1521) is the proposed Schedule S—the net savings deduction calculation. It arises from three decisions: the exclusion of borrowing from cash inflows, the exclusion of tax-exempt bond interest from cash inflows, and the exclusion of taxpayers with old wealth above $50,000 from the straightforward Domenici amortization method. The intention of the designers is to prevent households from using these sources of finance to take positive saving deductions when they are really not achieving any positive net saving.

How exactly does Schedule S work? It is too complex to describe here, or even in an endnote, in detail. But its purpose is easily understood. It is a complex set of taxpayer instructions that tries to prevent a household from obtaining a positive net saving deduction in a given year due the use of borrowed funds, tax-exempt bond interest, or old wealth, but permits these financing sources to reduce the dissaving of a dissaving household. The basic strategy is to create a special account that stores up these exclusions and deduction in years when the household is a positive saver for use in years when it is a negative saver.

Perhaps one may admire the heroic effort of the designers of Schedule S, given the problem created by the three decisions concerning borrowing, tax-exempt bond interest, and the old wealth of the affluent (over $50,000). Without Schedule S, these decisions would permit many taxpayers to claim large saving deductions even though they are not achieving any genuine positive net saving; these taxpayers would legally report a computed consumption that was substantially less than their actual consumption. Schedule S tries to stop this "abuse."

Unfortunately, it should be apparent that the Schedule S strategy generates the perverse incentive for a household to become a dissaver in order to use the stored up exclusions and deductions. I have already cited the criticisms of two professors of tax law concerning aspects of Schedule S: Warren (1995) on the treatment of borrowing and Kaplow (1995) on the treatment of old wealth. Perhaps the most comprehensive critique of Schedule S is provided by Ginsburg (1995) of the Georgetown University Law Center. After presenting a series of examples of the perverse taxpayer behavior and manipulations Schedule S would induce, he writes (p. 598):

All of these questions and concerns, all of the suggestions for manipulation set out earlier, and the many others that time and experience would bring forth, urge that Professor Warren's "tentative conclusions" concerning the superiority of a standard consumption tax model over the USA Tax's Unlimited Savings Allowance, and Professor Kaplow's determinations with regard to the recovery of preenactment basis, are absolutely correct. I would only add that conjoining tax-exempt bond interest with a savings deduction for the purchase of those bonds, as the USA Tax would do, seems to me genuinely flaky.

Not only does Schedule S generate perverse incentives; it is extremely complex and confusing. A labyrinth of taxpayer instructions must be followed before a household can determine whether its saving will be deductible this year. The opacity of Schedule S contrasts sharply with the clarity of the personal consumption tax return at the beginning of this chapter. On that return, the household adds its cash inflows, and subtracts nonconsumption cash outflows to compute its consumption this year.

Ginsburg ends his article positively (p. 598):

> In any event, a cash flow consumption tax that (1) includes borrowed amounts in the tax base and (2) does not hold the recovery of preenactment basis hostage to taxpayers' postenactment conduct, may not solve all of the problems and eliminate all of the opportunities real life and the tax bar can produce—the rich will persevere—but it will perform measurably better the task to which the Nunn-Domenici proposals are addressed.

I agree with Ginsburg. I have argued against all three decisions that led the designers to create Schedule S. Schedule S can be eliminated and the USA household tax becomes a genuine personal consumption tax if my three recommendations are followed: include borrowing (except for consumer durables) and tax-exempt interest in cash inflows and use the simple Domenici amortization method with a moderate ceiling for old wealth.

A related simplification concerns the use of "tax basis." Generally, "basis" is the cost of an asset. The word "basis" appears on many pages of the 1995 bill and 1995 Explanation. It is essential to Schedule S. Its use adds substantial complexity to the USA Tax. Under the approach I recommend, "basis" can be eliminated from the USA Tax except for the one-time computation of old wealth and for a small set of consumer durables that often appreciate in value such as housing (so that basis is needed to compute the capital gain). The virtual elimination of "basis" from the USA Tax would be a significant simplification.

Pension Funds

Under a personal consumption tax, there should be no special tax penalty for preretirement withdrawals from pension funds (in contrast to the current income tax) because the aim is to tax each household according to its consumption regardless of how it is financed—whether by "old" or "new" pension funds or any other source. I therefore recommend eliminating the current 10% penalty tax for all pension fund withdrawals. Although it might be tempting to retain the 10% penalty for preretirement withdrawal of "old" funds, it would be wrong in principle (each household should be taxed according to its consumption) and complex in practice (it would require households and pension managers to keep track of "old" versus "new" funds for many years).

With all saving tax deductible, pension fund saving will no longer possess a tax advantage over other saving. Employees will still find it convenient and advantageous to have their employer administer contributions to a pension fund, provided the fund permits preretirement withdrawals without restriction or penalty. Thus it is likely that most pension funds will remove these restrictions and penalties. The progressive tax rate schedule will still give the typical household an incentive to postpone withdrawal until retirement, when it is likely to be subject to a lower marginal tax rate.

The possibility has been raised (Steurle 1996; Bernheim 1996) that conversion to a personal consumption tax may reduce aggregate saving by reducing employer contributions to pension funds, and by removing restrictions and penalties on withdrawals from pension funds. It is suggested that employees may not have the self-discipline to save as much as employers saved for them through the current pension system, or to resist tapping their savings accounts and investment funds to finance preretirement consumption.

On the contrary, I suspect that pension fund saving may actually increase under a personal consumption tax. Most pension funds will probably remove restrictions and penalties on early withdrawals, and because of this removal, employees may support larger contributions. Administrative convenience will continue to give an advantage to employer-financed pension funds over individual saving. Today, employees hesitate to "lock up" too much wealth in a pension fund, and this hesitation limits employer contributions. But with restrictions and penalties removed, employees may desire larger pension contributions. Preretirement withdrawals may increase, but an increase in contributions may outweigh any increase in withdrawals.

But even if pension contributions decrease, the elimination of "lock up" should result in an increase in aggregate saving. Today, households can only get a tax deduction for saving by locking up their wealth until retirement. Under a personal consumption tax, a household can obtain a tax deduction for saving without locking up its wealth. This change is very likely to increase aggregate saving, even if pension saving declines.

Cash Hoarding Just Before Tax Conversion

Another transitional problem concerns hoarding cash just before tax conversion. Suppose a household sells financial assets or withdraws cash from savings accounts or investment funds and hoards the cash (in its home, in buried safety deposit boxes, in foreign or domestic "banks" that will not report cash withdrawals to the IRS, and so on). Then after tax conversion the household can finance consumption without paying tax by using its hoarded cash. If the assets would have been protected by the old wealth deduction described earlier, then nothing is gained by converting the assets to cash. But I have recommended protecting old wealth only up to a moderate ceiling. Thus there would be plenty to gain by converting unprotected assets to cash.

Cash hoarding is a transitional problem. As Graetz (1980, p. 274) writes: "Cash hoarding would be a problem only before the enactment of the expenditure tax. Subsequent to enactment, it would be to taxpayers' advantage to put cash into savings or investments, which would produce an immediate deduction."

But there is a problem with cash hoarding just before tax conversion. The objective here should be realistic. There is tax evasion under the personal income tax and there will be tax evasion under the personal consumption tax. Those who risk not reporting capital income under the income tax will risk not reporting hoarded cash. The objective is not to prevent evasion by experienced evaders, but to limit the number of new evaders.

Graetz's recommendation (1980, p. 274) seems sensible:

Initial cash balances should be included in receipts. To detect such cash, it would probably be necessary, as a practical matter, to rely on information reports of large withdrawals from savings accounts and of substantial sales of investment assets. Such detection would nevertheless be quite difficult.

As an aid to enforcement, it would probably be desirable to require taxpayers to file an initial report listing all assets on hand at the inception of the expenditure tax. If willful misstatements were subject to fraud penalties, truthful information would very likely be forthcoming.

Recall that to implement the old wealth deduction recommended earlier, each household must list all financial assets (and liabilities) it holds on December 31 prior to tax conversion. There is now a second reason for such a listing: limiting tax evasion. The household would be required to list cash held on December 31, and to include this amount in cash inflows on its first-year tax return. Experienced evaders will no doubt evade. It seems likely, however, that households too honest or risk-averse to evade under the income tax would generally be deterred by this requirement from attempting significant evasion through cash hoarding.

Phasing for Macroeconomic Stability

If the entire population were converted to the USA Tax in a single year, aggregate consumption growth in the economy might drop sharply below normal in response to the tax deductibility of saving. If so, there would be a temporary recession. Some analysts have ignored this risk because they doubt that the USA Tax will stimulate much saving. But the increase in saving may be larger than they think. In any case, because no one knows for certain, prudence warrants phasing in the USA Tax over perhaps half a decade.

There are at least four possible ways to phase in the USA Tax: (1) phase in the saving deduction for the whole population, (2) phase in the population by the household's adjusted gross income, (3) phase in the population by the age of the household's oldest member, and (4) phase in a representative cross-section of the population each year. I consider each in turn, and explain why I recommend cross-section phasing.

The first approach would be to convert the entire population in the same year, while phasing in the percentage of saving that can be deducted. For example, in year 1, only 20% of a household's saving would be deductible; in year 2, 40%; and so on. The advantage of this approach is that every household would be subject to the same personal tax system each year.

The disadvantage of this method is that more than just the percentage of saving that can be deducted would need to be phased in. A personal consumption tax should include changes other than a deduction for saving: the inclusion of borrowing, revenue from the sale of financial assets (not simply the capital gain), cash gifts and inheritances, and tax-exempt bond interest. Unless these are also phased in, the transition would be neither smooth nor fair. But with multiple phase-ins, it would be very hard to explain to a household the rationale for its tax in a transition year. Moreover, the IRS would have to cope with a change in rules for the entire population every year for half a decade; it would not fully administer the USA Tax until the half decade was over. This approach is therefore not recommended.

By contrast, the remaining options convert the population in stages. The disadvantage is that in every year only a percentage of the population has converted permanently to the USA Tax while the remaining percentage is still under the income tax. The advantage is that it is easy to explain to any household the rationale for its tax in a given year: either it is still being taxed on its income, or it is now being taxed on its consumption. Once the household converts to the USA Tax, it converts for life. Moreover, the IRS would have only two sets of rules throughout the half decade: the old income tax rules and the new USA Tax rules. It would begin to develop experience with the USA Tax rules in the first year with the initial 20% of the population that is converted in that year.

The second option phases in the population by the household's adjusted gross income (AGI). In year 1, households with an AGI in year 0 exceeding, say, $100,000 would be permanently converted to the USA Tax; in year 2, households with an AGI in year 1 exceeding $80,000 would be converted; and so on until year 5.

The third option phases in the population by the age of the household's oldest member. In year 1, households with the oldest member 30 or under would be permanently converted; in year 2, households with the oldest under 40; and so on until year 5.

The last option phases in a representative cross-section of the population each year. Each year a representative mix of incomes, ages, geographic location, and so on, would be converted. Once all household income tax returns of year 0 have been classified by these characteristics, the particular households chosen to convert each year could be selected by a random drawing.

Cross-section phasing has several advantages over the other two. First, no one can object that a particular income or age group is being favored or penalized. Second, converting a cross-section of the population each year should limit the harm to any particular industry. By contrast, under AGI phasing, each year the income class that just converted might cut its demand for particular products; for example, in year 1, the yacht industry might suffer a sharp cut in sales. Similarly, under age phasing, in year 1 the stereo industry might suffer a sharp cutback. But with cross-section phasing the newly converted in each year are a mixed group, so any change in demand will be spread evenly over all industries. I therefore recommend cross-section phasing over a half decade.

Business Tax Options

Many taxes can be levied on business firms. The USA Tax chooses a subtraction value-added tax (VAT) for its business tax. What is the rationale for this choice?

Recall what a subtraction VAT is. Each firm computes the difference between its sales revenue and its purchases from other firms, and applies a tax rate to this difference (approximately 11% for the USA Tax). In contrast to the corporate income tax, purchases of investment goods are fully deducted in the same year rather than depreciated gradually. This key feature makes the aggregate tax base for the whole business sector equal to value-added (output) minus investment, which equals consumption. By choosing a subtraction VAT for its business tax, the USA Tax has two components—household and business—with the same tax base: consumption. The business component is taxed at a flat rate (roughly 11%), while the household component is taxed at graduated rates.

Why a subtraction VAT instead of the credit-invoice VAT used by most other countries? With the credit-invoice method, each firm is taxed on its sales revenue, but is then given a credit for the VAT that has been paid by the firms from which it purchases. If the VAT tax rate is the same for all firms, the two methods are equivalent. For example, suppose firm A has sales revenue of $1,000 and purchases of $400. With an 11% subtraction VAT, its tax is 11% of $600 or $66. With an 11% credit-invoice VAT, its tax is 11% of $1,000 ($110) minus a credit of 11% of $400 ($44), or $66. Each type of VAT has its pros and cons (McLure 1987). Historically, in most European countries the credit-invoice VAT replaced the turnover tax—a sales taxes levied at all stages of production (manufacturing as well as retail). The credit-invoice VAT is a natural modification of the turnover tax. It continues to levy a tax on sales, but introduces a credit for tax paid at the earlier stage of production. Just as turnover tax rates often varied across commodity classes, the credit-invoice VAT can achieve varied rates by varying the retail stage sales tax rate.

By contrast, the USA VAT replaces the corporate income tax, which taxes the difference between sales revenue and certain expenses. The subtraction VAT is a natural modification of the corporate income tax. It continues to levy a tax on the difference between sales revenue and certain expenses—but now the deductible expenses include the purchase of investment goods, but exclude compensation, depreciation, and interest payments. Except for small corporations, the corporate rate is at least nominally uniform. The intent of the USA business tax is to maintain a uniform rate. Hence, starting with a turnover tax, the most natural VAT to choose is a credit-invoice VAT, while starting with a corporate income tax, the most natural VAT to choose is a subtraction VAT.

The flat tax is also a subtraction VAT except that each firm also deducts cash wages. Why not permit a deduction for wages under the USA business tax? Recall the reason for the flat tax wage deduction. Without it, the flat tax would be a one-component tax—a business subtraction VAT, which is simply a flat rate consumption tax on all households. It would have no progressivity; the tax burden on every household, rich or poor, would be the same percentage of its consumption. Flat tax advocates oppose progressivity at the top, but concede that there should be some protection at the bottom. This is the reason for the business cash wage deduction coupled with an individual wage tax with a large personal allowance.

But the USA Tax has a progressive household consumption tax with graduated rates; moreover, it retains the earned income tax credit for low-wage households and includes a new payroll tax credit. Hence there is no need to resort to a business cash wage deduction to protect low-income households. Thus it is better to keep the business tax a genuine VAT (no deduction for labor compensation). As a consequence, the USA business tax has a much larger tax base than the flat tax business tax, so that a lower tax rate can raise the same revenue. Moreover, far fewer firms will have a negative tax base, requiring carry-forwards.

A VAT excludes all financial payments and receipts (interest and dividends) except for financial institutions. The tax base equals revenue from the sale of real goods and services minus the purchase of real goods and services from other firms. By contrast, the corporate income tax includes interest but not dividends and may therefore distort the choice between debt and equity. This distortion could also be avoided by including all financial payments and receipts when computing the business tax base. The USA VAT opts for exclusion because it is simpler for nonfinancial firms. Financial institutions receive separate treatment.

The business firm is given a payroll tax credit, just as the household is given a payroll tax credit. Together, these credits remove the burden of the payroll tax without affecting Social Security finance. One objective of the USA Tax is to achieve a progressive federal tax system. In contrast to the flat tax, which ignores the large regressive burden of the payroll tax, the USA Tax provides credits for the payroll tax and preserves the earned income credit for low-wage workers.

According to Christian (1995, p. 376), the General Agreement on Tariffs and Trade (GATT) implies the following difference between the USA Tax and a flat tax: "Because the USA Tax allows no deduction for either direct or indirect compensation to employees, it is border adjustable for exports and imports. Because the flat tax allows a deduction for direct compensation, it is not border adjustable for exports and imports."

Because many of our trading partners have a VAT with border adjustability, the border adjustability of the USA business tax is desirable. Under the USA Tax, each firm excludes export sales but imports are taxed. Thus exports will leave the United States free of tax, and will then be subject to the VAT of the importing country. Symmetrically, imports that leave other countries tax-free will be subject to the USA business tax, just as U.S. firms are.

Should a firm be taxed according to the location of its official headquarters, or should it be taxed according the location of its production? Under the 1995 bill, the USA Tax is "territorial." It will tax only the net sales revenue of goods and services produced in the United States, whether by firms headquartered in the United States or in other countries.

Any business tax must handle a set of practical problems, such as the treatment of certain services, small enterprises and farmers, not-for-profit institutions, and housing and construction. VAT treatment of these issues has been thoroughly analyzed (McLure 1987), and the many countries with a VAT have experimented with various solutions. The USA business tax can call on this analysis and practical experience to handle these special problems.

Some transitional protection must be given. Consider the capital goods held by firms when tax conversion occurs. Under the income tax, firms did not deduct the purchase of these goods, but looked forward to deducting depreciation each year. Under the new USA Tax, new capital goods are deducted in the year of purchase, not depreciated gradually. But some depreciation of "old" capital goods should be permitted without sacrificing too much revenue. The 1995 bill includes such protection. The 1995 Explanation states (p. 1534): "The Business Tax adopts a compromise position between the two unacceptable extremes—(1) allowing all adjusted basis to be expensed in the first year or (2) prohibiting the deduction of any adjusted basis of old assets."

It is crucial to remember that the USA business tax is intended to raise only about 20% of USA Tax revenue while the household tax is to raise about 80%. Thus although both components of the USA Tax are important and must be consistent, the household tax is the major component. The fairness of the USA Tax system is controlled by the progressive household tax. The aim of the business tax is to remove the current bias against investment and reduce the extreme complexity of the current business tax: the corporate income tax. This it will surely do. The USA business tax is essentially a flat rate consumption tax. If it replaced the household tax, it would fail the test of progressivity and fairness. But together with a progressive household tax that raises 80% of the revenue, the business tax is a useful, consistent component of a progressive USA tax system.

Conclusion

Although the best way to handle certain practical problems has achieved a consensus among USA Tax designers, the best way to handle other practical problems remains unsettled. This chapter has described the major practical options and the solutions that have been proposed. It is crucial to emphasize that in some cases the proposed solutions are highly tentative and may well be modified as serious scrutiny and debate go forward and feedback continues to be received. I have argued that the USA household tax gets into practical difficulty to the degree it strays from its ideal: the personal consumption tax. I have therefore recommended that the USA household tax adhere to the ideal of a personal consumption tax in the details of its practical design.

5   Simplification

USA Tax advocates concede that their tax is not simpler than the sales tax, VAT, or flat tax. These taxes are not as simple as some advocates claim, but each is simpler than the USA Tax. This is no coincidence. USA Taxers believe that fairness requires that each household be taxed on its consumption at graduated rates, so that high consumers pay a significantly higher percentage than low consumers. It follows that the USA Tax has, as its main component, a household tax that computes household consumption. Such a tax cannot fit on a postcard.

USA Tax advocates, however, do claim that their tax, especially its business component, will turn out to be less complex in practice than the income tax. Of course it would be inappropriate to compare the current income tax, with its scars from years of lobbying and politics, to a pristine USA Tax. An enacted USA Tax will immediately begin to accumulate scars. Instead, USA Taxers claim that the inherent nature of the two taxes gives the USA Tax an advantage concerning complexity. To evaluate their argument, I begin with the household tax, then turn to the business tax, and finally address a phenomenon that plagues both components under the income tax: inflation. Because inflation is discussed last, zero inflation is initially assumed.

Throughout this book, I have argued that the USA household tax can be improved by adhering to the design of a progressive personal consumption tax, illustrated in the tax return presented in table 4.1. The argument has special force with respect to simplification. As explained in chapter 4, the 1995 USA Tax bill diverges from the consumption tax ideal in its treatment of borrowing, tax-exempt bond interest, and old wealth. This divergence led designers to create the complex and confusing Schedule S presented in the 1995 Explanation. Schedule S would prevent the USA household tax from being simpler than the household income tax.

Throughout this chapter, I assume that the decisions leading to Schedule S have been reversed, that Schedule S has been eliminated, and that the USA household tax adheres to the design of a personal consumption tax. A strong case can be made that such a tax would be somewhat simpler than the personal income tax.

Before focusing on the income tax, we note an important simplification concerning the estate and gift tax. In chapter 3, I argued that the basic principle behind a personal consumption tax implies that the estate and gift tax should be terminated. If we accept the principle that each person should be taxed according to his actual consumption—the resources he withdraws for his own benefit—then we should prefer a consumption tax to a consumption/gift/bequest (CGB) tax, and should favor ending the estate and gift tax because transfers of wealth do not entail actual consumption. Terminating the estate and gift tax (and replacing the revenue by raising consumption tax rates on the affluent) would achieve an important simplification in the U.S. tax system: all the complexity of estate tax planning techniques and regulations would be eliminated.

At the beginning of his *Harvard Law Review* article, Harvard professor of tax law William Andrews argues that tax simplification alone is a sufficient reason to convert the income tax to a personal consumption tax (1974, pp. 1115–1116):

If we think about the personal income tax in real terms, as a tax on accretion, and of accretion as consumption plus accumulation (or minus disaccumulation), reflection will show that its worst inequity, distortion, and complexity arise out of inconsistency in the treatment of accumulation. Under existing law, as we shall see, the effect is often to impair the integrity of the tax in relation to consumption as well as accumulation, so that some taxpayers with high standards of living pay limited taxes.

Why does this occur? Andrews explains that it is not lobbying and politics, but the inherent nature of accumulation that is at the root of income tax complexity:

But the underlying source of difficulty is with the accumulation component of accretion. Savings out of ordinary income are fully taxed, while accumulation of wealth in kind through appreciation in value of property already owned is not reflected in current taxable income. Further complications arise from this disparity. Some gains, though realized, are unrecognized by reason of special statutory provisions like those governing corporate reorganizations. These are among the most complex provisions in the statute, and have a substantial effect upon the structuring of financial transactions.... Wealth whose accumulation has already been taxed or permanently exempted is not to be taxed again, and so the statute has complex and imperfect provisions for computing and subtracting basis on sales, and for amortizing basis against ordinary income in the case of depreciable property. Distortions in the computation of depreciation and other items are sometimes grossly magnified by the way borrowing is treated in the case of leveraged investments, so that a limited passive investment may produce an artificial loss which shelters other income from tax even though that other income remains freely available for current consumption or other investments.

So what should be done about these income tax complexities? Andrews continues (p. 1116):

The way out of these difficulties, according to the accretion ideal, is to make taxable income provide a more comprehensive reflection of real accumulation, and therefore accretion, by including unrealized changes in the value of property in taxable income. Literal achievement of that goal would require that all assets be taken into account at current fair market value at the end of each accounting period. Although practical exigencies may prevent comprehensive inclusion of unrealized appreciation, improvement is thought to lie in that direction.

Another remedy for present difficulties lies in just the other direction. It involves putting the income tax treatment of business and investment transactions more completely on a simple cash flow basis. Investment expenditures would be deductible when made; on the other hand, all receipts from business and investment activities, including loan proceeds, would be immediately and fully includable in taxable income. This would have the effect of treating accumulation consistently by excluding it from taxable income even when it is represented by investment of realized gains or of ordinary income.

Similarly, Bradford (1980, pp. 80–81) argues that tax simplification is an important reason to convert:

When turning from definition to practical implementation, one might expect consumption to pose greater problems than income (since one normally reckons consumption by subtracting savings from income). Yet I shall argue here that precisely the opposite is the case: a consumption tax can be readily constructed on the basis of current-year cash transactions only, virtually all of them also used in an income tax, while dispensing with the elements of income calculation that are based on transactions in the (sometimes distant) past and are designed to approximate unobservable quantities. These account for many of the most irksome features of income taxation in practice.

Kay and King, who contributed to the Meade Commission report (Institute for Fiscal Studies 1978), believe a personal consumption (expenditure) tax is simpler than an income tax. Recall that the commission concluded that important benefits would be gained by conversion to an expenditure (personal consumption) tax. In their text on the

British tax system, Kay and King write (1990, p. 99): "One advantage of choosing consumption expenditure as the tax base is that we require no valuations of an individual's wealth, and hence we avoid all the problems of measuring depreciation of assets, of indexing for inflation, and of our inability to measure some important components of wealth, such as pension rights or human capital."

They emphasize the advantage of a cash flow tax (p. 113):

> The simplification involved in moving from an income basis to an expenditure base arise principally from the shift from an accruals base to a cash-flow base. It does not matter whether a receipt is an item of capital or income. It is unnecessary to determine the date of the transaction to which any particular item relates; the issue is simply when and whether a particular cash payment occurred. Every question on the expenditure tax (ET) form asks only about actual cash payments that took place during the year of assessment.

A Simpler Household Tax

USA Tax advocates claim that three complex aspects of the income tax would become simple under the household consumption tax: capital gains, employee compensation, and saving.

Capital Gains

USA Taxers argue that capital gains is simple under their tax. The USA household tax return strategy is to follow the cash in order to compute consumption. Revenue from the sale of stock must be included in cash inflows. Any stock not sold for cash is irrelevant. This year's cash purchase of stock is deductible saving (a cash outflow not used for consumption), while any past purchase is irrelevant.

But capital gains is far from simple under the income tax. Income tax advocates generally assert that capital gains should be treated like any other income. But in practice it can't be done, not because of lobbying and politics, but because of its inherent nature. Most economists agree that a capital gain—a rise in the market value of stock—is income whether "realized" or not through the actual sale of stock. But most acknowledge that in practice it is necessary to defer tax until the stock is actually sold. Finally, most agree that there is no simple, practical way to "make up" for the deferral: a simple treatment results in unfairness and inefficiency, while even a complex treatment cannot fully eradicate these defects.

Why is capital gains a serious problem for the income tax? Consider a simple example. Initially assume there is no economy-wide inflation and no income tax. Suppose on January 1 a household takes $100,000 from its bank account and buys corporate stock for $100,000; and that on December 31 it sells the stock for $105,000, returns $100,000 to its bank account, and deposits $5,000 in a separate "income" account where it also deposits its paychecks that come to $50,000 for the year. This year the household could consume $55,000 while preserving its $100,000 bank account. Most economists therefore agree that its income is $55,000. Note that its income has two components: $50,000 of labor income and $5,000 of capital gains income.

Now consider one little change to our example. Suppose the household doesn't actually sell the stock on December 31, though it could have sold it for $105,000. Does this decision change its income? Most economists say, "No." Because it could have sold the stock and consumed $55,000 while keeping its bank account at $100,000, most economists agree that its income is $55,000. Economists generally define income as the maximum consumption the household could have enjoyed this year ($55,000) while leaving its wealth ($100,000) unchanged. Most economists therefore agree that, whether the stock is sold or not, this household has $55,000 of income.[1]

But under the income tax of virtually all countries including the United States, the household's tax depends on whether it sells the stock. If it doesn't sell, tax is deferred. Economists recognize that there are good practical reasons for deferring tax until the stock is actually sold. For example, the market value of unsold stock is not always known; its value on December 31 may be the result of a sudden fluctuation in the stock market, and the household may be short of cash. So tax is deferred to the year of sale, when the household must pay tax on the difference between the sales revenue and the cost of the stock. This treatment is simple, but completely unsatisfactory. Why?

If the stock were sold on December 31, the $5,000 would have been taxed immediately. For example, at a 28% rate the household would have kept $3,600. With an annual 5% return in a bank account that is taxed annually at 28%, its after-tax return would be 3.6%. In twenty years, it would accumulate $7,303 in its account to finance consumption.[2] But if the stock is not sold for twenty years, gains 5% in value each year and pays no dividends so that its annual return is also 5% (just like the bank account), it would be sold for $13,267 in year 20,[3] and after a tax of $2,315 (28% of the capital gain of $8,267) could finance $10,952 of consumption (50% more than $7,303).

So this treatment is simple but unsatisfactory. How you save, and whether or not you sell your stock, determines how much tax you pay and how much consumption you can ultimately finance. Households are biased toward one kind of saving and against others; and they feel "locked in" to the stocks they own. The result is unfair, and the lock-in is inefficient for the economy.

Can't we make up for deferral in the year of sale by charging a higher tax? The trouble is that the correct tax depends on when and how the stock rose in value over the twenty years, and we cannot expect households to keep track of this. Hence any practical deferral penalty formula would be incorrect and unfair for many households.

Unfortunately, the inability to tax capital gains properly is not a minor defect of an income tax. Many affluent households finance a significant fraction of their consumption with capital gains. Deferral confers a benefit not available to wage earners. At the same time, not all the affluent benefit from capital gains. Hence there is also an inequity among the affluent.

Recall from chapter 3 that USA Taxers claim that the treatment of capital gains is fair and efficient as well as simple under their tax. Any household financing high consumption with capital gains pays a high tax because revenue from the sale of stock is included. But a household that refrains from consuming its capital gains pays no tax. By contrast, the income tax permits an affluent household to enjoy high consumption yet pay low tax if it is financed by capital gains; at the same time, the tax causes a lock-in effect and a disincentive to save.

Employee Compensation

USA Taxers argue that employee compensation is simpler under their tax. Because household consumption is computed from household cash flows, the USA Tax ignores compensation in the form of stock dividends, stock options, pension contributions, or the accumulation of defined benefit pension credits. Only when cash is actually withdrawn by the household from any of these sources of compensation is it included in the computation of consumption.[4]

But compensation is complex under the income tax. Suppose that instead of raising cash salary from $50,000 to $55,000, an employer gives an employee stock with a market value of $5,000 on the date given, or the option to buy stock at a price $5,000 less than its market value during a specified period, or an increment in its defined benefit pension with a present value of $5,000. Most economists agree that all of these are current income.

But none of these entails the immediate payment of cash to the employee and none is fully equivalent to a $5,000 cash payment. The stock may rise or fall in value as soon as it is given. The option may have to be exercised by a particular date and require a cash expenditure by the employee. The promise of the pension benefit may not be fulfilled, and the interest rate appropriate to compute its present value can be debated. Thus treating each as equivalent to $5,000 cash salary is not really satisfactory, yet ignoring such compensation is even less so.

The current income tax struggles with these forms of compensation (Phillips and Cramer 1993). A stock dividend is usually nontaxable. Some stock options receive capital gains treatment: no tax is due when the option is granted or exercised, and capital gains tax is due if and when the stock is sold. Other stock options may be taxed when granted if the stock has a readily ascertainable fair market value; if not, it is taxed as ordinary income if and when the employee exercises the option to buy the stock, and a capital gains tax is due if and when the stock is sold. Pensions are untaxed until benefits are paid.

Under the income tax the form of compensation determines its tax treatment, and the tax treatment often diverges from that prescribed by an ideal income tax. The problem here is not lobbying or politics. It is the inherent nature of these forms of income.

Saving

USA Taxers argue that household saving is simple under their tax. All saving for any purpose in any form in any amount is excluded from the tax base. If the saving entails an outflow of cash by the household (i.e., the purchase of stock), it is deducted. If the saving entails a rise in the market value of an asset that is not sold, it never enters the cash flow computation of consumption. But saving is complex under an income tax. First consider saving under an ideal income tax, and next, saving under the actual income tax.

Under an ideal income tax, all income should be taxed, whether the income is consumed or saved. But this requires taxing forms of saved income that have no cash transaction, such as unrealized capital gains and employee noncash compensation. Thus successfully implementing an ideal income tax is unfeasible. Purely due to practical obstacles, some forms of saved income must remain untaxed.

Now turn to the current income tax. Its treatment of saving is even more complex. Why? Because many citizens apparently reject the ideal of an income tax when it comes to retirement saving. An employer contribution to a defined contribution pension fund entails a cash transaction that could easily be imputed to the employee and taxed. But the citizenry seems to want this income that is saved for retirement to be excluded. The individual retirement account (IRA) is a specific deduction for retirement saving. Favored tax treatment is given to Keogh, 401(k), and tax-sheltered annuity plans. The tax guide I use (Bernstein 1995) devotes 50 pages in a 500-page book to the complex rules governing these favored saving vehicles. USA Taxers point out that the chapter would disappear under their tax.

A Simpler Business Tax

USA Taxers argue that their business tax—a subtraction VAT—is much simpler than the corporate income tax. The reason is not lobbying and politics, but the inherent nature of what each attempts to tax. Measuring the annual net income of a business is difficult. The corporate income tax attempts to do so. The subtraction VAT does not. Instead, the subtraction VAT taxes net cash flow for goods and services. The tax is levied on cash inflow from sales minus cash outflow for purchases from other firms (including investment goods). For the whole business sector, the aggregate tax base therefore equals gross value added minus gross investment, which equals consumption.

USA Taxers point to two complex aspects of the corporate income tax that would become very simple under the business subtraction VAT: depreciation, and debt versus equity financing.

Depreciation

Depreciation is irrelevant to the USA business tax base. The expenditure on an investment good is deducted immediately—"expensed." The subtraction VAT does not attempt to measure the annual net income of the firm; hence, it does not require a measure of depreciation.

By contrast, the corporate income tax requires each firm to try to measure its annual net income. To do so, it must measure the cost of goods sold in a given year. This includes the economic depreciation of real capital that year. But such depreciation has no cash transaction. It must be estimated. Firms must be given a rule that prescribes the amount it can deduct for depreciation.

If the rule is kept simple, then the deduction permitted will be greater than true economic depreciation for certain capital goods, and smaller for others. This disparity will give firms an artificial incentive to purchase certain capital goods and not others. In some industries, the rule will underestimate economic depreciation, so that net income is overestimated and overtaxed; in other industries, the rule will overestimate economic depreciation, so that net income is underestimated and undertaxed. The result will be a misallocation of capital across industries; capital will flow from industries with high marginal productivity to industries with low marginal productivity solely because of the defective depreciation rule.

Of course, an attempt can be made to reduce this economic waste by making the depreciation rule very complex, assigning each capital good to an appropriate asset category, and trying to prescribe an economically accurate depreciation rule for each category. This approach requires the IRS to utilize studies that try to estimate the depreciation pattern for many types of capital goods. But there is no guarantee that even a complex rule based on such studies will significantly reduce the misallocation of capital. The result may well be to add a lot of complexity without reducing waste very much.

Debt versus Equity

Under the USA business tax, cash inflows from debt or equity financing, and cash outflows to pay interest or dividends, are irrelevant to the tax base (except for financial institutions).[5] Hence there is no bias for or against debt or equity because the choice of finance is irrelevant to the tax base.

By contrast, the corporate income tax in principle includes a deduction for the cost of capital and labor in the cost of goods sold in a given year. But the current corporate income tax permits a deduction for the cost of debt capital—interest payments—but not for the cost of equity capital. Why the disparate treatment?

One reason is that the cash cost of debt capital is not at the firm's discretion, while the cash cost of equity capital is. A firm must pay the agreed upon cash interest, but can adjust the cash dividend. True, rules might be prescribed by which the firm would estimate the cost of its equity capital, regardless of its actual dividends. But the current corporate income tax rejects such an estimation; it simply does not allow any deduction for the cost of equity capital. Although this is a simple solution, it biases the corporation toward debt and against equity financing.

Inflation

USA Taxers argue that inflation is simple under their tax. Both the household and business taxes use current cash flows to compute the tax base. Inflation causes a serious problem whenever there is a need to compare current cash flows with past cash flows. But such a need generally does not arise under the USA Tax. By contrast, the income tax is plagued by the need to make such comparisons. USA Taxers point to two prime examples: capital gains under the household income tax and depreciation under the corporate income tax.

Inflation and Capital Gains

It is impractical to tax unrealized capital gains annually. Under the current income tax, tax is deferred until the stock is sold. In the year of sale, the gain is computed by subtracting a past cash flow (the purchase price) from a current cash flow (the sales price). If many years have elapsed, even a low inflation rate will substantially distort the comparison of the current cash flow and the past cash flow.

For example, consider stock bought twenty years ago for $1,000 and sold today for $1,806. If the annual inflation rate were only 3% during the twenty years, then the $1,806 today has no greater purchasing power over real goods and services than the $1,000 did twenty years ago.[6] Yet under the current income tax, the household would owe tax this year on $806. Nominal income, computed by combining current and past cash flows, enters the tax base, rather than real (inflation-adjusted) income.

Inflation and Depreciation

It is impractical to accurately measure economic depreciation annually. Under the current corporate income tax, a rule prescribes how much a firm can deduct for depreciation of a particular capital good. The deduction is based on the purchase price of the good and its assigned asset life. For example, if the good cost $1,000 and its assigned asset life is twenty years, then if the straight-line depreciation rule is used, $50 can be deducted each year.

Suppose this capital good is still in service in its twentieth year, but inflation has been 3% annually over its life. Then the capital good might cost $1,806 if it were bought today, and corresponding depreciation would be about $90 (1.806 x $50). Revenue today from goods produced by this capital good would be about 1.806 times the revenue from the same goods twenty years ago. Yet under the current corporate income tax, the corporation would only be able to deduct $50 this year. Clearly, this combination of current and past cash flows distorts the measure of the firm's net income.

Can the Inflation Distortion Be Removed?

It might seem easy to remove the inflation distortion under the income tax. For capital gains and depreciation, the purchase price could be adjusted upward by the amount of inflation so that current dollar revenue is combined with an inflation-adjusted purchase price. In the capital gains example, $1,806 rather than $1,000 would be subtracted from the sales price of the stock. In the depreciation example, $90 rather than $50 would be deducted.

In fact, removing the inflation distortion would be difficult for this reason: the inflation adjustment must be comprehensive—applying to all items distorted by inflation—to improve efficiency. Adjusting some items, but not others, might increase total distortion. In particular, it is crucial that inflation-adjusted interest expenses, rather than nominal interest expenses, be made deductible. Why?

Suppose that with zero inflation a person has an opportunity to buy $1,000 of stock that will yield a 4% capital gain, but must borrow at 5% interest. The person will turn it down, and this is economically efficient; funds should be allocated to another firm that can generate a higher return on its investment.

With 3% inflation, the nominal capital gain and the nominal interest expense will be roughly 3% higher (7% and 8% respectively). If the capital gain is adjusted for inflation, then only 4% or $40 will be subject to tax; if the marginal tax rate is 40%, the tax is $16 and the person keeps $54 ($70 – $16). If the interest expense were also adjusted for inflation, then only 5% or $50 would be deductible, yielding a tax saving of $20 so the interest cost would be \$60 (\$80 − \$20). With a benefit of \$54 and a cost of \$60, again the person would turn it down, and this is economically efficient.

But if nominal interest were still deductible, then 8% or \$80 would be deductible, yielding a tax saving of \$32 so the interest cost would be only \$48 (\$80 − \$32). With a benefit of \$54 and a cost of \$48, the person would now decide to buy the stock. Funds would be channeled into an investment that is economically inefficient. Thus adjusting capital gains without adjusting interest expenses would introduce a powerful new source of inefficiency into the economy.

McLure, who supervised the 1984 "Treasury I" tax reform proposal, which included inflation adjustment, later expressed his pessimism about its feasibility to a National Tax Association meeting (1988, p. 308):

There are basically two satisfactory approaches to dealing with the need for inflation adjustment. One is to adjust selected items in the income statement used to calculate taxable income, such as interest income and expense, the basis of capital assets used in calculating gains and losses, the basis of depreciable (and similar) assets, and the cost of goods from inventories. This is the approach followed in Treasury I. This form of inflation adjustment is unlikely to be totally comprehensive, if only because it is unlikely that adjustments would be made for financial claims such as money that do not bear interest, or indeed, for any financial asset yielding an interest rate below the inflation rate.

A more comprehensive approach, which is used in Chile, would make adjustments to the balance sheet and then recognize them in the calculation of income. Though this approach produces a much more accurate measure of income, it is significantly more complicated than the approach based on adjustment of income items, in part because it involves adjustment of balance sheets. In fact, it is likely that ad hoc measures would be used for most individuals, with the comprehensive approach being applied only to large businesses and perhaps wealthy individuals.

There is no need to focus on the details of these two approaches. The important lesson for the present purpose is that inflation adjustment would add appreciably to the complexity of the income tax, especially if the basic income tax is flawed (in the sense that it would not produce an accurate measure of income even in the absence of inflation). The thought of adding inflation adjustment to rules such as those for interest allocation and the limitation of deductions for passive losses would presumably strike fear in the hearts of many in this room.

The Inherent Complexity of the Income Tax

In his advocacy of conversion to a cash flow consumption tax on practical grounds, Andrews (1974, p. 1140) writes:

But many of the most intractable problems in the personal income tax arise directly out of the hybrid character of our treatment of accumulation. The complexities of corporate distributions and reorganizations, for example, at the individual taxpayer level, all have to do with matters discussed here: realization and nonrecognition, basis determination and recovery, capital gain or ordinary income treatment, and treatment of debt. Other seemingly simpler provisions, like that governing installment sales, have essentially to do with deferral or nonrecognition. The trust and partnership provisions involve complex problems of defining when gain will be recognized by individuals and whether it will be capital gain or ordinary income. The partnership provisions, in particular, have very complex provisions concerning the determination and recovery of basis, and the treatment of partnership borrowing. The whole matter of qualified pension and profit-sharing plans is primarily one of deferral, and other compensation schemes, like stock option plans, are designed to defer recognition of gain and to secure capital gain treatment when recognition occurs. Most of the problems that occupy most of the time of tax practitioners and administrators (not to speak of teachers, students, legislators, and taxpayers themselves) arise immediately out of our failure to take a consistent and comprehensive position with respect to inclusion or exclusion of real accumulation in taxable income.

In his recollection of his attempt at the Treasury to reform the income tax, McLure (1988, pp. 304–307) writes:

I want to focus on the complexity that is inherent in any attempt to tax all real economic income uniformly and consistently and then suggest that maybe we should begin to think seriously about an alternative form of direct taxation based on consumption, rather than on income...

We sometimes hear someone say about a particular tax provision that "It is only a matter of timing," meaning that the same amount of tax will be paid, only later (or sooner). Such a statement reveals a basic failure to understand—or a desire that others not understand—the nature of income taxation and tax avoidance. The income tax is, in theory, applied annually to income from business and capital as it accrues. If income tax can be postponed, interest (or other capital income) can be earned on a tax deferred basis in the meantime. The attention paid to such provisions as those for depreciation allowances is strong testimony to the fact that much of tax planning and lobbying in the arena of tax legislation is based on this simple truth...

Ultimately, in attempting to handle these and other timing issues satisfactorily, one creates a system that, in principle, measures income fairly accurately, but is hopelessly complex. And that is before we consider inflation adjustment!

Tax Simplification in Perspective

Given the assault that USA Taxers mount against the complexity of the income tax, it is important to repeat their concession that the USA Tax is not the simplest available tax. The chapter on practical options reveals

several problems that will cause some complexity even if they are opti-
mally treated. Eliminating Schedule S will greatly simplify the USA Tax,
and should be the highest priority for USA Tax designers; but its elimination will not remove all complexity. Finally, lobbying and politics are
bound to take some toll on an enacted USA Tax.

The central aim of most USA advocates is not simplification, but raising national saving and investment without sacrificing progressivity.
Most USA Taxers make a modest claim about simplification. They
argue only that the USA Tax, especially its business component, will
turn out to be less complex in practice than the income tax. Their claim
about the household component is hollow if Schedule S remains, so that
the USA household tax diverges from a personal consumption tax. But if
the decisions leading to Schedule S are reversed and Schedule S is eliminated, a strong case can be made that the resulting personal consumption tax will, on balance, be simpler than the personal income tax.

Why is it called the "USA" Tax?

Under the USA Tax, each household is given an unlimited savings allowance. This means that each household can deduct all saving, without any limit, for any purpose, in contrast to the limited, restricted, complex retirement saving deductions of the current income tax.

What is the USA Tax?

The USA Tax consists of two components: a household tax and a business tax. The household tax replaces the current household income tax. The business tax replaces the corporate income tax and applies to all businesses, not just corporations. The household tax will raise roughly 80% of the revenue, the business tax, 20%; these are the same proportions as the current income tax.

The USA household tax takes as its ideal the progressive personal consumption tax. It makes all household saving deductible—it gives each household an unlimited savings allowance; by contrast, under the income tax, saving deductions are limited, restricted, complex, and linked to retirement.

The USA business tax takes as its ideal the consumption-type, subtraction value-added tax (VAT). It makes all business investment in capital goods (such as machinery and computers) immediately deductible in the year of purchase; by contrast, under the current income tax, business investment must be gradually deducted over the life of the goods ("depreciated"). These are significant changes from the current income tax.

Is the USA household tax a progressive personal consumption tax?

Yes. Each household is taxed according to its consumption (at graduated rates) because all saving is deductible. On the annual household tax return (due April 15) of a personal consumption tax, each household adds its cash inflows (wages and salaries, interest and dividends, revenue from the sale of stocks and bonds, etc.) and then deducts all nonconsumption cash outflows; what is left is consumption. After taking personal exemptions and a family allowance, the household applies the rates in the tax table to its taxable consumption to obtain its tentative tax (under the USA Tax, it then takes a new payroll tax credit and possibly the earned income tax credit to obtain its actual net tax).

The 1995 USA bill does differ in certain details from a personal consumption tax. One theme of this book is that the USA Tax generally gets into trouble when it strays from the design of a personal consumption tax. I therefore recommend amending the 1995 bill to adhere to the design of a personal consumption tax.

Doesn't the USA Tax favor the affluent who can afford to save most?

No. The USA household tax (which raises 80% of USA tax revenue) is a progressive consumption tax with graduated rates that are adjusted to make each income class pay roughly the same total tax revenue that it pays under the current income tax.

True, if the tax rates were not adjusted—if the USA Tax simply used the current income tax rates and bracket amounts—then the USA Tax would indeed favor the affluent. The affluent would take large saving deductions, thereby enjoying a large tax cut, while many low-income households might be unable to afford any saving deduction, and would therefore pay the same tax. But then the government would collect less total revenue and our budget deficit would get even worse. So tax rates must be adjusted to keep total tax revenue roughly the same.

Once the need to adjust tax rates is grasped, it is obvious how this can be done to avoid favoring the affluent. Because the affluent can afford to save most, their tax rates must be raised most in order to keep the total tax dollars they pay the same; and since low-income households save least, their tax rates must be raised least (perhaps not at all) in order to keep the total tax dollars they pay the same. This is exactly what the USA Tax does. Thus not only does the USA Tax raise the same total revenue, it raises the same revenue from each income class.

Of course, this doesn't mean that each individual household will pay the same tax. Within each income class, households with above-average saving will pay less tax, while households with below-average saving will pay more tax. The income class as a whole will pay the same total tax revenue. This is one reason the USA Tax should raise total saving: within each income class, it will leave more after-tax income in the hands of high-saving households.

By contrast, all other consumption taxes do indeed favor the affluent who can afford to save most. The sales tax and the VAT are levied entirely on firms that pass on the burden to consumers through higher prices. These taxes cannot vary the tax rate according to each household's level of consumption. The flat tax raises roughly half its revenue from its business tax. Even the half that comes from its household tax does not use a set of graduated rates. All other consumption taxes shift the tax burden from the affluent to the nonaffluent.

Most advocates of other consumption taxes believe this shift is fair because they regard the current burden on economically successful households as excessive and unfair. USA Tax advocates believe the current distribution of the tax burden is reasonably fair, and shifting it away from the affluent would be unfair, especially because of the recent rise in the inequality of earnings.

Thus the USA Tax is a consumption tax that utilizes graduated rates to achieve significant progressivity and to make sure that the tax burden is not shifted from the affluent to the nonaffluent, in contrast to all other consumption taxes.

What is the purpose of the USA Tax?

The main purpose is to raise the saving (investment) rate of the U.S. economy without sacrificing progressivity and fairness. The United States has been a very low saving (investment) nation by international standards for several decades. Of the twenty-three OECD nations, the United States has ranked twentieth in its gross saving rate since the 1960s; its gross saving rate has been only half the rate of the leader, Japan. Moreover, our net saving rate has been declining, from 9% in the 1970s to 5% in the 1980s to 3% thus far in the 1990s. Because saving is necessary to finance investment in plant, equipment, and technology, most economists agree that if our saving rate remains much lower than other economically advanced nations, eventually we will produce less output per person, and experience a lower standard of living, than these nations.

Are we saving too little, or are other countries saving too much?

A good case can be made that we are saving too little. Our saving rate is not the result of individual choice in an undistorted free market. Our income tax discourages saving by making saving nondeductible, yet taxing the return to saving—capital income (interest, dividends, and capital gains). Our social insurance programs (Social Security, Medicare, and unemployment insurance), while providing valuable insurance protection and peace of mind, have the negative side effect of giving people an incentive to save less. Federal budget deficits reduce national saving, but do not necessarily reflect the choice of individual citizens. Moreover, a higher saving rate would generate "public goods" that citizens value—a higher international ranking, faster poverty reduction for low-wage workers, and a greater contribution to "the ascent of man" through technological progress; yet each individual has no incentive to save for these public goods. Thus a strong case can be made that we are saving too little for our own well-being.

Is the USA Tax the only tax that encourages saving?

No. There are other taxes that would also promote saving and invest-ment—a national sales tax, a value-added tax, and a flat tax. But each is much less progressive than the current income tax; they would all entail a huge tax cut for the affluent and a tax increase for the nonaffluent. Their advocates believe this would be fair; USA Tax advocates don't. By contrast, the USA Tax uses graduated rates, the earned income tax cred-it, and a new payroll tax credit to maintain progressivity while promot-ing saving and investment.

Will the USA Tax really raise saving?

The USA Tax is very likely to raise saving for three reasons: the incentive effect, the horizontal redistribution (heterogeneity) effect, and the post-ponement effect. Consider each in turn. Each person has a greater

incentive to save because all saving is now deductible. Among the affluent class, high savers will enjoy a tax cut and more disposable income,
while low savers will suffer a tax increase and have less disposable
income; this horizontal redistribution of disposable income from low to
high savers should result in more total saving from the affluent. Finally,
some tax is postponed to the retirement stage of life when consumption
often exceeds income, enabling people to save more during their work
stage.

Today under the income tax, a household must be willing to "lock
up" its saving until retirement to obtain a tax advantage. By contrast,
under the personal consumption tax, a household can obtain a tax
deduction for saving without submitting to a "lock up." Every year
when a household looks at its tax return, it will receive a simple message from the IRS: "All saving for any purpose in any amount is tax
deductible." As households come to grasp this simple new message, it
seems likely that aggregate saving will increase.

How much better off will we be if we raise our saving rate?

It is estimated that gradually raising our gross private saving rate from
15% to 18% will eventually raise output per person 10% and consumption per person (the standard of living) 6% above what they would
have been in every future year. Of course, in the short run we will sacrifice, but the sacrifice will be modest and will last less than a decade.
After that we will be permanently better off. The rate of return on our
sacrifice will be roughly 13%. Within two decades, the wage of low-
educated workers will be 4% higher and the wage of high-educated
workers, 9% higher than they would have been.

But won't an increase in the saving rate cause a recession?

Not if its done gradually. Today, real output, consumption, and investment all normally grow about 2.5% per year. We envision a half-decade
transition during which consumer goods production grows more slowly
(say 1.5%) and investment goods production grows more rapidly (say
6%) so that output growth stays at its normal 2.5%, thereby maintaining
a constant unemployment rate. Fewer jobs will open up in the consumer
goods sector, but more jobs will open up in the investment goods sector,
so some workers will switch sectors while remaining employed.

At the end of the half decade, investment (private plus government) will be a larger share of total output (say 24% instead of 20%) and consumption will be a smaller share (say 76% instead of 80%). Thereafter, both consumer goods and investment goods can grow at the same rate—a rate that will be a bit faster than 2.5% for many years because of the higher capital stock that is achieved by fast investment growth during the transition.

During the half decade, the USA Tax induces the slower consumption growth and the Federal Reserve induces the faster investment growth. The Fed does it by reducing interest rates enough to induce business managers to increase their orders of investment goods, thereby stimulating faster investment goods production. Total demand (consumption plus investment) and hence total output will continue to grow at its normal 2.5%, thereby maintaining a constant unemployment rate and avoiding recession.

Clearly, the USA Tax must be phased in gradually to make sure that consumption growth declines modestly but remains positive (say from 2.5% to 1.5%). Methods for phasing in the USA Tax were discussed in chapter 4.

Is the USA Tax better than the income tax?

Here's why USA Taxers believe it is. The USA Tax encourages saving and investment, while the income tax does not. On the household tax return, all saving is deductible under the USA Tax, while only some retirement saving is deductible under the current income tax (and none would be deductible under a true income tax); some investment in human capital (higher education tuition) is deductible under the USA Tax, while none is deductible under the income tax. On the business tax return, all investment is immediately deductible under the USA Tax, while investment can only be gradually depreciated under the income tax. Thus the USA Tax should achieve a higher saving (investment) rate for the economy, and therefore a higher future standard of living.

The USA Tax overcomes an important conflict that plagues the income tax. Under the income tax, advocates of saving often propose reducing the tax rate on certain kinds of capital income, such as capital gains. Many object that this would allow affluent high consumers to pay little tax if their consumption is financed by capital gains. But under the USA Tax, high consumers always pay high tax, however their consumption is financed, but all households are encouraged to save by the saving deduction.

USA Taxers argue that it is fairer to tax each household according to what it takes out of the economic pie for its own enjoyment—its consumption—rather than what it contributes to the economic pie through its output, which is roughly measured by its income. The USA Tax taxes each household on its consumption (at progressive rates), not its income.

Consumption is a better measure of ability to pay than income for retirees, who often have significant wealth but low income. True, consumption is not a better measure of ability to pay for misers, but there are surely more retirees than misers. Besides, misers take little out of the economic pie, leaving most of the resources they could have consumed for others to consume or businesses to invest.

Is the USA tax better than a national sales tax or a VAT?

Here's why USA Taxers believe it is. The USA Tax is progressive, while the national sales tax and value-added tax are not. The USA Tax is progressive for three reasons. First, it uses a set of graduated rates—rates that rise with the level of household consumption. Second, it retains the earned income tax credit for low-income households. Third, it introduces a new payroll tax credit to offset the burden of the FICA Social Security tax on low-income households.

By contrast, the sales tax and VAT implicitly charge the same percentage at the cash register to all households (the tax is included in the price); for example, if the tax rate is 20%, then every household bears a burden equal to 20% of its consumption, whether it is affluent or poor. True, a sales tax or VAT might try to reduce the burden on low-income households by various methods. But either tax will redistribute the tax burden from the affluent to the nonaffluent, as shown in chapter 3.

Is the USA Tax better than the flat tax?

Here's why USA Taxers believe it is. Though the flat tax is mildly progressive, the USA tax is much more progressive for three reasons. First, it uses a set of graduated rates—rates that rise with the level of household consumption. Second, it retains the earned income tax credit for low-income households. Third, it introduces a new payroll tax credit to offset the burden of the FICA Social Security tax on low-income households.

True, the flat tax achieves some protection at the bottom through the personal allowance for low-income households. But the protection is less than the USA Tax, which retains the earned income credit and introduces a new payroll tax credit for these households.

Progressivity is much greater at the top for the USA Tax because the flat tax uses a single rate (roughly 20%) above its family allowance for all households, while the USA Tax uses a set of graduated rates like the current income tax. For example, the U.S. Treasury estimates that the richest 1% (with income over $349,000 in 1996) would enjoy a huge 36% tax cut upon conversion to the flat tax; the richest 5% (income over $145,000), 21%; the richest 10% (income over $109,000), 14%. Because the flat tax must try to raise the same revenue as the income tax, nonaffluent households would suffer a tax increase. By contrast, USA graduated rates are set to raise roughly the same total revenue from the affluent and nonaffluent as the current income tax; affluent high savers will pay less tax, but affluent low savers will pay more tax.

The USA household tax return will probably appear fairer to many citizens than the flat tax household return. The USA household return requires inclusion of all cash inflows—whether from capital or labor; all sources of financing consumption are included. By contrast, the flat tax household return omits all capital income. Although flat tax advocates argue that capital income has already been taxed at its source—the business firm—many citizens will feel that if the household return includes labor income, it should also include capital income, so that such income can be taxed progressively rather than at a single rate at its source.

Are any taxes deductible?

No, for three reasons. First, taxes are often consumption outflows—they often finance the consumption of public services. Second, this treatment avoids distorting the choice of taxes by state and local governments. Third, citizens will bear the full cost of state and local government services, so they will weigh full cost against benefit when they vote on public services.

What saving is deductible?

All saving: cash deposits into any saving account or investment fund, purchase of stocks or bonds, or household contributions to a pension fund, retirement fund, or life insurance. If the USA Tax is amended so that it taxes each household on its consumption, then all nonconsumption cash outflows (except taxes paid or withheld) would be deductible. For example, purchase of real estate property (nondeductible under the 1995 bill) would be deductible (except for owner-occupied housing, which would be treated like other consumer durables, as explained below).

Must the household include changes in the market value of its investment fund on its tax return?

No. Only cash deposits to and withdrawals from the investment fund enter the household tax return. The strategy of the household return is to follow the cash. Cash inflows are added and cash outflows for saving are subtracted. What's left must have gone to finance consumption. So only actual household cash flows are relevant. Fluctuations in portfolio values are not.

Are USA household tax rates too high?

USA tax rates are set to raise the same total revenue as the current income tax, and to achieve the same distribution of the tax burden across income classes. Because of the saving deduction, tax rates must be higher than under the income tax to achieve the same revenue. The discrepancy is small for nonaffluent households that save little, but is larger for affluent households that, on average, save an important fraction of their income.

Somewhat higher tax rates may have some discouraging effect on persons working to finance current consumption. But persons working for future consumption may be encouraged by the deferral of tax to later in life. And persons working to provide security for their heirs through gifts and bequests should be encouraged by the deferral of tax until their heirs actually consume.

Because of the new payroll tax credit, a USA tax rate of 40% has the same effect as a 32.35% income tax rate (32.35% = 40% − 7.65%, where 7.65% is the employee payroll tax rate). Suppose a person with income less than the payroll tax ceiling ($61,200 in 1995) earns another $100 of wage income and saves none of it. Under a 7.65% payroll tax and a 32.35% income tax rate, the person would pay $32.35 in income tax and $7.65 in payroll tax, or $40 in tax, keeping $60. Under a 40% USA tax rate, the person would pay $7.65 in payroll tax and due to the credit, only $32.35 in USA net tax, or $40 in tax, keeping $60. Thus due to the payroll tax credit, USA Tax rates have the same effect as income tax rates 7.65% lower (for persons below the payroll tax ceiling).

Is the USA Tax a new idea?

No. The idea of taxing each household according to its consumption rather than income has been advocated by distinguished economists for a half century. In the 1970s, two reports—the U.S. Treasury's *Blueprints for Basic Tax Reform* and the Institute for Fiscal Studies' *The Structure and Reform of Direct Taxation*—concluded that a household consumption (expenditure) tax is practical and desirable. Since the 1970s, many economists have supported conversion of the income tax to a personal consumption tax, including David Bradford (Princeton), Martin Feldstein (Harvard), Lester Thurow (MIT), Lawrence Summers (Harvard), Michael Boskin (Stanford), and Kenneth Arrow (Stanford).

Is the USA Tax a partisan idea?

The 1995 USA Tax bill was introduced in the Senate by Republican Domenici and Democrats Nunn and Kerrey. Of the economists listed above as supporters, some are conservative and some are liberal. This is no accident. The USA Tax encourages saving and investment without altering the degree of progressivity of the tax system. By contrast, all the other consumption tax proposals—sales tax, VAT (as a replacement for the entire income tax system), and flat tax—are likely to be partisan and politically divisive because they would greatly reduce the progressivity of the tax system.

Is the USA household tax really a wage (labor income) tax?

No. The USA household tax is a progressive consumption tax. Each household adds all cash inflows including wages, interest, dividends, and revenue from the sale of stocks and bonds, and then deducts cash outflows for saving. The household is therefore taxed according to its consumption, not according to its wage (labor) income.

The easiest way to see that the USA Tax is not a wage tax is to consider a notorious character: the lazy heir. The lazy heir inherits a large fortune, uses it to finance a high level of annual consumption, and never works a day in his life. Under a wage (labor income) tax, the lazy heir would owe zero tax every year. But under the USA Tax, every year the lazy heir would owe a high tax because of his high consumption. Each year, the lazy heir would sell stocks and bonds, or simply withdraw cash from some fund, to finance his consumption. Under the USA Tax, he would be required to add these cash inflows on his tax return. With no offsetting saving deduction, he would be taxed on these cash inflows that measure his consumption.

So why does anyone allege that the USA Tax is really a wage (labor income) tax? There is one similarity. Both a consumption tax and a wage tax remove the discouragement to saving imposed by an income tax. The consumption tax permits a deduction for saving in the year it occurs; the income tax does not. The wage tax permits an exemption of capital income (interest, dividends, capital gains); the income tax does not. Both taxes therefore raise the reward to saving.

Some opponents pounce on this similarity to declare that any consumption tax is "really" a wage tax. This is a clever tactic, because most citizens recoil at the unfairness of a wage tax, asking, "Why should a household with a low wage but high consumption pay a low tax?" Why, indeed? In fact, this is one reason the flat tax may repel many citizens once they actually look at its postcard return and see a line for wage income but no line for investment income.

So let's advance the debate by recognizing that though wage and consumption taxes are similar in one respect, they are surely not the same. Just ask the lazy heir.

What happens to the capital gains controversy under the USA Tax?

It disappears. Under the income tax, one side argues that capital gains income should be taxed at a lower rate to promote saving and investment. The other side argues that this would be unfair because it would permit some of the affluent to enjoy high consumption while paying little tax. Hence there is political deadlock.

Conversion to the USA Tax would break the capital gains deadlock. Under its household consumption tax, income from whatever source is never taxed per se. It is only taxed, and always taxed, if it is consumed. Thus, revenue from the sale of stock is added to cash inflows on the tax return. If it is matched by equal saving, none of it is consumed so none of it is taxed; if none of it is saved, all of it is consumed so all of it is taxed. And consumption, however financed, is always taxed at graduated rates.

How are gifts and bequests treated?

Under a personal consumption tax, a donor should not be taxed on gifts or bequests given because these cash outflows do not entail an actual withdrawal of resources by the donor for his own enjoyment. To measure a household's actual consumption, all cash inflows should be summed, including gifts and bequests received; and all nonconsumption cash outflows should be subtracted, including cash gifts and bequests given. Moreover, if we accept the principle that each person should be taxed on what he actually withdraws from the economic pie for his own benefit, then the estate and gift tax should be eliminated because these transfers of wealth do not entail actual consumption (the revenue should be replaced by raising personal consumption tax rates on the affluent).

The 1995 USA bill does not follow this treatment. Under the 1995 bill, gifts and bequests are ignored—the same treatment as the current income tax. The donor cannot deduct a gift and the donee excludes it. The 1995 bill proposes no change in the estate and gift tax. The 1995 bill does follow proper consumption tax treatment in one respect: the final tax return does not tax the donor on his accumulated wealth that he leaves as a bequest.

Are most consumer durables taxed in the year of purchase?

Yes. Because expenditure on the typical durable is nondeductible, it is in effect taxed in the year of purchase. Of course, a durable that costs $1,000 really yields a smaller amount of consumption each year of its life. So this treatment is called "tax prepayment": too much tax is paid in the year of purchase and too little (none) in each subsequent year. It evens out, yet keeps things simple.

Are there any exceptions for consumer durables?

Yes. If a loan is secured by and used to purchase a durable (such as an auto loan), then tax on the amount of the purchase equal to the loan is spread over time. This is easily implemented simply by ignoring the loan and subsequent repayments in the household's annual tax computation: instead of including the loan as a cash inflow, it would be excluded; instead of permitting loan repayments to be deductible, they would be nondeductible. The loan exclusion exempts this amount from tax in the year of purchase; the nondeductibility of repayments in effect taxes the repayments in each subsequent year.

There may be one exception to this nondeductibility of loan repayments. Under the 1995 USA Tax bill, home mortgage interest payments are deductible (principal payments are not deductible), as under the current income tax. It should be noted that under that 1995 bill, property taxes are not deductible (no taxes are deductible), the entire capital gain is taxed when the homeowner sells the home and becomes a renter (the current income tax exclusion of $125,000 of the capital gain is terminated), and home equity loan interest is nondeductible.

It is important to emphasize that spreading cannot be achieved under a sales tax or VAT because they lack a household tax return. The flat tax has a household tax return, but its advocates reject loan spreading to keep it as simple as possible. So the USA Tax is the only consumption tax that spreads the tax burden of durables over time.

Is there any relief for "old" wealth from double taxation?

Yes. Moreover, the USA Tax is the only consumption tax that provides some relief. Consider someone who has accumulated "old" wealth after paying income tax. If the income tax were retained, the person would be able to consume this old wealth tax-free. But unless special relief is given, this consumption will be taxed. For example, under a sales, value-added, or flat tax, this person will bear the tax through a higher price for consumer goods.

Under the 1995 USA Tax bill, households with previously taxed old wealth of $50,000 or less would be permitted to deduct 100% of their old wealth over three years. Instead, I recommend that the following schedule apply to the old wealth of all households: 80% of the first $50,000, 40% of the next $50,000, and 0% thereafter; then 20% of this deductible old wealth would be deducted for each of five years. The aim is to strike a balance between fairness and simplicity.

What would happen to pension funds?

An important advantage of a personal consumption tax over the current income tax is that all saving in any form will receive the same tax treatment in order to compute consumption accurately: all saving will be deductible because it is a nonconsumption cash outflow, and all withdrawals from any fund will be included in cash inflows without any special tax penalty. The fifty pages in the tax guide book I use that are devoted to the varying income tax treatment of alternative savings vehicles will disappear.

Thus pension funds will no longer possess a special tax advantage over other saving. Nor will there be a special tax penalty for preretirement withdrawals from pension funds. Although employees may still want their employer to administer contributions to a pension fund, it is doubtful that employees will be happy with a pension fund that prohibits or penalizes preretirement withdrawals. It therefore seems likely that most pension funds will eventually remove these restrictions and penalties.

Although some analysts believe pension funds will decrease, they may actually grow. Administrative convenience will still favor employer-financed pension funds. With restrictions and penalties removed, employees may support larger pension contributions. But whether pensions grow or decline, the opportunity to obtain a saving deduction without locking up wealth until retirement should cause households to raise aggregate saving.

Is the USA Tax unfair to the young and the old?

No, answer USA Taxers. The young will not have to pay the whole tax on "big ticket" items (house, car) in the year of purchase—the tax will be spread over time if it is financed by a loan. Today's elderly will be given some relief from double taxation through an old wealth deduction. Future elderly will pay more tax because they will pay less tax during middle-age years due to the deduction for saving.

Is the USA Tax more complex than the income tax?

No, answer USA Taxers. Its household tax is simpler with respect to capital gains, employee compensation, and saving; its business tax is simpler with respect to depreciation, and debt versus equity financing; and both are simpler with respect to inflation.

Capital gains is simple under the USA Tax. Because the aim is to compute consumption by following this year's cash flow, revenue from the sale of stock is included in cash inflows, but any stock not sold for cash is irrelevant and any past purchase is irrelevant.

Employee compensation is simpler under the USA Tax. Since consumption is computed from household cash flows, there is no need to consider stock dividends, stock options, pension contributions, or the accumulation of defined benefit pension credits.

Saving is simple under the USA Tax. All saving for any purpose in any form in any amount is excluded from the tax base. There is no need to determine the tax treatment of a particular saving vehicle (IRA, Keogh plan, pension fund, and so on).

Depreciation is irrelevant to the USA business tax. The expenditure on an investment good is deducted immediately—"expensed." Cash flows from debt or equity financing are irrelevant to the tax base (except for financial institutions), hence there is no bias toward debt or equity.

Inflation is simple under both household and business taxes. Because both use current cash flows to compute the tax base, there is no need to compare past dollars with present dollars during an inflationary period—in sharp contrast to the income tax, where such comparisons are frequent.

The 1995 version of the USA Tax needs to be simplified. If borrowing (except for a specific consumer durable) is included in cash inflows and repayments are deductible, if state and local bond interest is included in cash inflows, and if old wealth is handled as recommended by Domenici (1994), then the complex and confusing Schedule S (presented in the 1995 Explanation) can be eliminated, greatly simplifying the USA Tax.

What is the USA business tax?

The business tax is a subtraction value-added tax (VAT). It replaces the corporate income tax and applies to all business firms. Each firm would be taxed roughly 11% on the difference between its sales revenue and its purchases from other firms, including capital goods. Its most important feature is that expenditure on capital goods would be immediately deducted instead of gradually deducted (depreciated) over time as under the current income tax.

How does the USA business tax differ from the corporate income tax?

Here are the differences. First, the USA business tax applies to all businesses, not just corporations; this broadens the tax base and enables a lower tax rate. Second, capital goods are immediately deducted rather than gradually deducted (depreciated), thereby encouraging investment. Third, the tax is border- adjustable—export sales are excluded and imports are taxed; this enables proper integration with the border-adjustable VATs of our trading partners. Fourth, employee compensation is not deductible; this raises the tax base and enables a lower tax rate. Fifth, financial transactions are ignored; interest and dividends received are excluded, and there is no deduction for either interest or dividends paid. This removes the current bias toward debt financing under the income tax, where interest is deductible but dividends are not. Sixth, cash flow accounting is used rather than more complex accrual accounting. Seventh, the tax is territorial—only goods produced in the United States are subject to tax; this eliminates the complexity of accounting for foreign subsidiaries. Eighth, the USA business tax is much simpler than the corporate income tax because of most of the differences just cited.

Can the design of the USA Tax be improved?

Yes. My basic recommendation is that the USA household tax should adhere to its ideal—the personal consumption tax. It should instruct the household to add all cash inflows, then subtract all nonconsumption cash outflows (except taxes withheld or paid) in order to compute its taxable consumption.

Borrowing should be included in cash inflows and repayments should be deductible as a nonconsumption cash outflow. The exception is borrowing to finance a specific durable; in this case each year's consumption is better measured by excluding the loan and making the repayments nondeductible. State and local bond interest, and cash gifts and inheritances received, should be included in cash inflows. The double taxation of old wealth should be limited by a relatively simple method that applies to all households (Domenici 1994), rather than the complex method proposed in the 1995 bill for households with old wealth over $50,000.

The language and exposition of the USA household tax should reflect the fact that it is a personal consumption tax, not a personal income tax. The items added on the tax return should be called cash inflows, not gross income; the items subtracted should be called non-consumption cash outflows, not net saving. The result should be called taxable consumption, not taxable income.

There is no harm in using a title that tells what is not taxed: saving. But there should be no attempt to conceal what is taxed: consumption. After all, there is a strong case to be made that a progressive personal consumption tax is the fairest tax, because it charges each household according to what it withdraws from the economic pie for its own enjoyment, rather than what it contributes to the pie. Moreover, the percentage each household is charged rises with its consumption.

Nor should it be claimed that the USA Tax taxes all income once. In truth, the USA Tax taxes consumption twice, once at the business level at a low flat rate, and once at the household level at a set of higher graduated rates.

In sum, the USA Tax will be simpler, fairer, and more compelling if its designers convey clearly that it is a progressive consumption tax, not an income tax, and if they remain faithful to this fact in all details of design, implementation, and exposition.

Notes

Chapter 1

1. Economists who have written in support of the personal consumption tax include Irving Fisher (Yale), Nicholas Kaldor (Cambridge), James Meade (Cambridge), David Bradford (Princeton), Martin Feldstein (Harvard), Kenneth Arrow (Stanford), Lawrence Summers (Harvard), Lester Thurow (MIT), Mervyn King (London School of Economics), and Michael Boskin (Stanford).

2. $30,000 and 20% are approximate.

3. Fisher and Fisher, *Constructive Income Taxation* (1942). Kaldor's *An Expenditure Tax* (1955) advanced the case for a household expenditure tax, but serious practical work did not occur until the 1970s with the U.S. Treasury's *Blueprints for Basic Tax Reform* (1977) and the Institute for Fiscal Studies' *The Structure and Reform of Direct Taxation* (1978), along with two detailed *Harvard Law Review* articles by Andrews (1974) and Graetz (1979).

4. For example, suppose the household's USA Tax is $5,000. If its payroll tax is $4,000, the household will receive a $4,000 credit so that its USA net tax—the check it writes to the IRS—is only $1,000. If its payroll tax is $6,000, the household will receive a $6,000 credit so that it obtains a USA refund of $1,000 from the IRS (the payroll tax credit is "refundable"). In either case, the household's total tax is $5,000, just as specified by the USA Tax schedule. The Social Security system is unaffected.

5. For example, suppose the business firm's USA Tax is $5,000. If its payroll tax is $4,000, the business will receive a $4,000 credit so that its USA net tax—the check the business writes to the IRS—is only $1,000. If its payroll tax is $6,000, the business will receive a $6,000 credit so that its net tax this year is $0 and it carries forward a $1,000 credit to next year. In either case, the business's total burden is $5,000, just as specified by the USA Tax schedule. The Social Security system is unaffected.

Chapter 2

1. To see this, suppose in year 0 that output is 100, consumption 80, and investment 20. If consumption grows 1.5% per year for five years, in year 5 it will be $80 \times (1.015)^5 = 86$. If investment grows 6.2% per year for five years, in year 5 it will be $20 \times (1.062)^5 = 27$. So output in year 5 will be $86 + 27 = 113$; hence output will have grown approximately 2.5% per year because $100 \times (1.025)^5 = 113$. But now consumption will be 76% of output ($86/113 =$

0.76) and investment will be 24% of output (27/113 = 0.24). From then on, we envision the shares (76%, 24%) remaining constant so that output, consumption, and investment all grow at the same rate—a bit higher than 2.5% per year for many years due to the greater investment share (24% versus 20%).

Chapter 3

1. Recall our discussion in chapter 1 of Hite and Roberts's (1991) survey of a sample of taxpayers reported by Sheffrin (1993), which provides evidence that the majority of Americans believe that significantly graduated income tax rates are fair.

2. Suppose the firm would pay a wage of $16,000 if it cannot deduct the wage. Then if it can deduct the wage, it would pay a wage of $20,000, thereby saving $4,000 in tax, again for a cost of $16,000; but the employee would pay $4,000 in tax, again keeping $16,000. Because the firm's wage cost is the same in both cases, its prices would be the same to consumers. Either way, the employee has $16,000 to spend and faces the same product prices, and the government obtains $4,000 in tax.

3. Instead of having $16,000 to spend, as it would under a 20% VAT, it has $20,000, yet faces the same product prices.

4. Flat tax revenue would be $615.5 billion compared to income tax revenue of $753.8 billion (81.6%).

5. OTA's table includes these footnotes:

(1) This table distributes the estimated change in after-tax income due to the proposal with a revenue-neutral rate of 20.8 percent (approximately).

(2) Family Economic Income (FEI) is a broad-based income concept. FEI is constructed by adding to AGI unreported and underreported income; IRA and Keogh deductions; nontaxable transfer payments, such as Social Security and AFDC; employer-provided fringe benefits; inside build-up on pensions, IRAs, Keoghs, and life insurance; tax-exempt interest; and imputed rent on owner-occupied housing. Capital gains are computed on an accrual basis, adjusted for inflation to the extent reliable data allow. Inflation losses of lenders are subtracted and of borrowers are added. There is also an adjustment for accelerated depreciation of noncorporate business. FEI is shown on a family, rather than on a tax return basis. The economic incomes of all members of a family unit are added to arrive at the family's economic income used in the distributions.

(3) The taxes included are individual and corporate income, payroll (Social Security and unemployment), and excises. Estate and gift taxes and customs duties are excluded. The individual income tax is assumed to be borne by payors, the corporate income tax by capital income generally, payroll taxes (employer and employee shares) by labor (wages and self-employment income), excises on purchases by individuals by the purchaser, and excises on purchases by business in proportion to total consumption expenditures. Taxes due to provisions that expire in the budget period are excluded.

(4) The change in federal taxes is estimated at 1996 income levels but assuming fully phased-in law and static behavior. The incidence assumptions for the repealed income taxes is the same as for the current law taxes. The flat tax on wages (plus pension benefits received) is assumed to be borne by wages plus pension benefits received in excess of the standard deduction. The flat tax on the labor component of self-employment income is assumed to be borne by that income. The flat and excise taxes on employer-provided fringe benefits (except pension contributions) and the flat tax on payroll taxes are

assumed to be borne by employees in proportion to benefits or taxes. The flat tax on business cash flow (which excludes the labor component of self-employment income) is assumed to be borne by capital income generally.

(5) The standard deduction is $21,400 (joint) or $10,700 (single) plus $5,000 for each dependent. The flat tax on the labor component of self-employment income is included in this column.

(6) The proposal would disallow a deduction for employer-provided fringe benefits (except pension contributions) making these benefits (primarily employer-provided health insurance) subject to the 20.8 percent flat tax and would impose an equivalent excise tax on such benefits provided by governments and nonprofit organizations. The employer portion of payroll taxes would likewise be nondeductible.

(7) The proposal, in total, is shown here to reduce after-tax income (increase taxes) because the distributions exclude the effect of the Armey proposal to repeal the estate and gift taxes and the income tax on fiduciaries.

(8) Families with negative incomes are excluded from the lowest quintile but included in the total line.

Note: Quintiles begin at FEI of Second $15,604; Third $29,717; Fourth $48,660; Highest $79,056; Top 10 percent $108,704; Top 5 percent $145,412; Top 1 percent $349,438.

6. OTA assumes labor supply is inelastic (unresponsive to a change in the wage), so that workers bear the entire burden of any labor tax, whether legally levied on the employer or employee.

7. The OTA describes its methodology as follows: "No attempt is made in this analysis to estimate the tax-induced behavioral responses of either individuals or corporations. Following the standard revenue-estimating conventions used by both the Office of Tax Analysis and the Joint Committee on Taxation, the macroeconomic aggregates, such as the level of compensation, prices, employment, and gross domestic product, have been assumed to be unchanged by the proposal."

8. Economists agree that it is a mistake to claim that consuming will benefit others by creating jobs or income, because the jobs and income can be just as readily created by firms ordering plant, equipment, and technology—by investing—as by households' consuming. The real issue is whether resources will be released to benefit others.

9. Suppose the wage is $30,000 and the consumption tax rate that applies to income minus saving is 20%. Then C pays a tax of $6,000 in period 0, and $0 in period 1, for a lifetime tax of $6,000. Assume S saves $10,000 in period 0, and with a 50% interest rate, accumulates $15,000 for withdrawal in period 1. Then S pays a tax of $4,000 in period 0 (20% of [$30,000 − $10,000] and $3,000 in period 1 (20% of $15,000, because capital income is $5,000 and saving is −$10,000, so income minus saving is $15,000). The present value of this $3,000 tax is $2,000 ($3,000/1.5). Thus S's lifetime tax (present value of taxes in the two periods) equals $6,000 ($4,000 + $2,000), so C and S pay the same lifetime tax under the consumption tax.

10. Actually, Aaron and Galper support a compromise. They would tax gifts and bequests only above a high lifetime exemption, so the wealthy donor pays tax but the average donor pays none. They write (1985, p. 68):

It is desirable to permit each person to make some additional personal gifts or bequests free of tax. For example, moderate transfers between parents or children at time of need and other modest intrafamily gifts or bequests should not be made into taxable events. Sizeable exemptions are undesirable, because they would result in unequal taxes on people with similar lifetime spending capacities. But a lifetime exemption of $100,000 per person [nearly $200,000 in 1996], $200,000 per couple [nearly $400,000 in 1996] would permit most families to exclude all gifts and bequests from tax without materially eroding the principle that total spending capacity should be taxed in full; most wealth transferred between generations is concentrated in estates larger than these limits.

11. Some analysts concede that the lazy heir shows that a consumption tax is not equivalent to a wage tax; but they instead claim it is equivalent to "an endowment tax." An endowment tax is a tax on wages, inheritances, and gifts received; it would therefore require the lazy heir to pay a large tax upon receipt of the large inheritance. Still, a progressive consumption tax differs from an endowment tax because it taxes each household annually according to its actual annual consumption, and it scales the progressivity to actual annual consumption, not to the annual endowment. Graetz (1980) emphasizes the difference between a progressive consumption tax and an endowment tax.

Chapter 4

1. Note that $20\% = 25\%/[1 + 25\%]$; more generally, $t_i = t_e/(1 + t_e)$.

2. Owner-occupied land and housing is discussed below under consumer durables.

3. The $4,559 is obtained from the standard amortization formula, $\mathbf{a} = rP/\{(1 + r) - [1/(1 + r)^{T-1}]\}$. If $r = 7\%$, $T = 5$, and $L = \$20,000$, then $\mathbf{a} = \$4,559$. The formula is obtained by solving for $\mathbf{a}$ in $L = a + [a/(1 + r)] + [a/(1 + r)^2]...[a/(1 + r)^{T-1}]$, which states that the loan L equals the present value of the annual payments $\mathbf{a}$.

4. Of course, the definition of "independent household," "external," and "internal" is not always obvious and defining the borderlines would involve some ingenuity and care. But often the distinction is obvious and clear-cut. For example, gifts or bequests to children who have not yet completed secondary school should be "internal" and have no tax consequences.

5. It should be noted that neither Domenici (1994) nor the 1995 USA Tax bill proposes the termination of estate and gift taxes.

6. Although Aaron and Galper (1985) favor the CGB tax (which they call a cash flow income tax) in principle, in practice they would only tax the gifts and bequests of wealthy donors.

7. The donor received a deduction for the purchase of stocks or bonds in the year of purchase, because this was necessary to compute the donor's consumption in that year. If the stocks or bonds were purchased prior to enactment of the personal consumption tax, this should be handled by the treatment of "old wealth," discussed later.

8. If the donor bought the stock prior to enactment, this raises the issue of the proper treatment of "old wealth," discussed later.

9. Such a ceiling implies that tuition above $10,000 is 100% consumption. This is surely conservative.

10. If there were universal national health insurance that limited out-of-pocket medical expenses to a designated percentage of household income (Seidman 1994b, 1995; Feldstein and Gruber 1995), then a deduction under the USA Tax would be unnecessary.

11. Note that if the household sold the stock for $150,000, it would have been taxed on the $100,000 capital gain under the income tax, so only $50,000 would have been tax-free.

12. If by taking its deduction a household would compute a negative amount for taxable consumption, the IRS should send it a check equal to the lowest bracket percentage times this amount. If the standard carry-forward procedure were used instead, these households might be tempted to raise consumption in order to be able to use their maximum deduction immediately rather than wait. An immediate check would avoid such a temptation.

Chapter 5

1. Equivalently, economists define income as actual consumption plus the change in wealth (net worth). For example, suppose this household actually consumed $45,000, and increased its bank account by $10,000. Then its income is $55,000.

2. $\$3,600 \times (1.036)^{20} = \$7,303$.

3. $\$5,000 \times (1.05)^{20} = \$13,267$.

4. Chapter 4 ("Practical Options") discussed several cases where household consumption does not entail a household cash outflow (for example, employer-financed health insurance or employer provision of recreation facilities), and prescribed treatment. Because these are also problems for the income tax, they are not discussed here.

5. A special set of rules is prescribed for financial institutions.

6. $\$1,000 \times (1.03)^{20} = \$1,806$.

7. Capital gain would be relevant to the USA Tax only for a small set of consumer durables such as housing (as explained in chapter 4).

References

Aaron, Henry J., and Harvey Galper. 1985. *Assessing Tax Reform.* Washington, D.C.: Brookings Institution.

Andrews, William D. 1974. A Consumption-Type or Cash Flow Personal Income Tax. *Harvard Law Review* 87, no.6 (April): 1113–1188.

Auerbach, Alan J., and Laurence J. Kotlikoff. 1987. *Dynamic Fiscal Policy.* Cambridge: Cambridge University Press.

Bernheim, B. Douglas. 1996. *Rethinking Saving Incentives.* Department of Economics Working Paper, Stanford University.

Bernstein, Allen. 1995. *1996 Tax Guide for College Teachers.* Washington, D.C.: Academic Information Services.

Boskin, Michael J. 1984. Saving Incentives: The Role of Tax Policy. In *New Directions in Federal Tax Policy for the 1980s,* ed. Charls E. Walker and Mark A. Bloomfield, 93–111. Cambridge, MA: Ballinger.

Bradford, David F. 1980. The Case for a Personal Consumption Tax. In *What Should Be Taxed: Income or Expenditure?,* ed. Joseph A. Pechman, 75–113. Washington, D.C.: Brookings Institution.

Bradford, David F. 1986. *Untangling the Income Tax.* Cambridge, MA: Harvard University Press.

Bradford, David F. 1987. On the Incidence of Consumption Taxes. In *The Consumption Tax: A Better Alternative?,* ed. Charls E. Walker and Mark A. Bloomfield, 243–261. Cambridge, MA: Ballinger.

Burtless, Gary. 1996. Worsening American Income Inequality. *Brookings Review* 14, no.2 (spring): 26–31.

Center for Strategic and International Studies. 1992. *Strengthening of America Commission: First Report.* Washington, D.C.: CSIS.

Christian, Ernest S. 1995. The Tax Restructuring Phenomenon: Analytical Principles and Political Equation. *National Tax Journal* 48, no.3 (September): 373–385.

Christian, Ernest S., and George J. Schutzer. 1995. USA Tax System: Description and Explanation of the Unlimited Savings Allowance Income Tax System. *Tax Notes* 66, no.11 (March 10), Special Supplement: 1482–1575.

Committee on Ways and Means, U.S. House of Representatives. 1993. *Green Book.* Washington, D.C.: U.S. Government Printing Office.

Congressional Budget Office. 1994. *An Economic Analysis of the Revenue Provisions of OBRA-93.* January.

Council of Economic Advisors. 1992, 1996. *Economic Report of the President.* Washington, D.C.: U.S. Government Printing Office.

Courant, Paul, and Edward Gramlich. 1984. The Expenditure Tax: Has the Idea's Time Finally Come? In *Tax Policy: New Directions and Possibilities,* 27–35. Washington, D.C.: Center for National Policy.

Domenici, Pete V. 1994. The Unamerican Spirit of the Federal Income Tax. *Harvard Journal on Legislation* 31, no.2 (summer): 273–320.

Domenici, Pete, Sam Nunn, and Bob Kerrey. 1995. S. 722: USA Tax Act of 1995.

Engen, Eric M., William G. Gale, and John Karl Scholz. 1994. Do Saving Incentives Work? *Brookings Papers on Economic Activity* no.1: 85–151.

Feldstein, Martin. 1976. Taxing Consumption. *The New Republic* (February 28): 14–17.

Feldstein, Martin, and Jonathan Gruber. 1995. A Major Risk Approach to Health Insurance Reform. In *Tax Policy and the Economy* 9, ed. James M. Poterba, 103–130. Cambridge, MA: MIT Press.

Fisher, Irving, and Herbert W. Fisher. 1942. *Constructive Income Taxation.* New York: Harper and Brothers.

Fisher, Ronald C. 1996. *State and Local Public Finance* (2d ed.). Chicago: Irwin.

Frank, Robert H., and Philip J. Cook. 1995. *The Winner-Take-All Society.* New York: Free Press.

Ginsburg, Martin D. 1995. Life under a Personal Consumption Tax: Some Thoughts on Working, Saving, and Consuming in Nunn-Domenici's Tax World. *National Tax Journal* 48, no.4 (December): 585–602.

Goode, Richard. 1980. The Superiority of the Income Tax. In *What Should Be Taxed: Income or Expenditure?,* ed. Joseph A. Pechman, 49–73. Washington, D.C.: Brookings Institution.

Gottschalk, Peter. 1993. Changes in Inequality of Family Income in Seven Industrialized Countries. *American Economic Review Papers and Proceedings* 83, no.2 (May): 136–142.

Graetz, Michael J. 1979. Implementing a Progressive Consumption Tax. *Harvard Law Review* 92, no.8 (June): 1575–1661.

Graetz, Michael J. 1980. Expenditure Tax Design. In *What Should Be Taxed: Income or Expenditure?,* ed. Joseph A. Pechman, 161–276. Washington, D.C.: Brookings Institution.

Hall, Robert E., and Alvin Rabushka. 1983. *Low Tax, Simple Tax, Flat Tax.* New York: McGraw-Hill.

Hall, Robert E., and Alvin Rabushka. 1985. *The Flat Tax.* Stanford, CA: Hoover Institution.

Hall, Robert E., and Alvin Rabushka. 1995. *The Flat Tax* (2d ed). Stanford, CA: Hoover Institution.

Hite, Peggy A., and Michael R. Roberts. 1991. An Experimental Investigation of Taxpayer Judgments on Rate Structures in the Individual Income Tax System. *Journal of the American Tax Association* (fall): 47–63.

Institute for Fiscal Studies. 1978. *The Structure and Reform of Direct Taxation.* London: George Allen and Unwin.

Kaldor, Nicholas. 1955. *An Expenditure Tax.* London: George Allen and Unwin (reprinted by Greenwood Press, Westport, CT, 1977).

Kaplow, Louis. 1995. Recovery of Pre-Enactment Basis under a Consumption Tax: The USA Tax System. *Tax Notes* 68, no.9 (August 28): 1109–1118.

Kay, John A., and Mervyn A. King. 1990. *The British Tax System* (5th ed). Oxford: Oxford University Press.

Levy, Frank, and Richard J. Murnane. 1992. U.S. Earnings Levels and Earnings Inequality: A Review of Recent Trends and Proposed Explanations. *Journal of Economic Literature* 30, no.3 (September): 1333–1381.

Lewis, Kenneth A., and Laurence S. Seidman. 1991a. The Quantitative Consequences of Raising the U.S. Saving Rate. *Review of Economics and Statistics* 73, no.3 (August): 471–479.

Lewis, Kenneth A., and Laurence S. Seidman. 1991b. The Transition Path in a Growth Model: The Sato Controversy Revisited. *Journal of Macroeconomics* 13, no.3 (summer): 553–562.

Lewis, Kenneth A., and Laurence S. Seidman. 1993. The Impact of Raising the U.S. Investment Rate on the Wage of Low-Educated Labor. *Journal of Macroeconomics* 15, no. 3 (summer): 511–520.

Lewis, Kenneth A., and Laurence S. Seidman. 1994. A Phased Increase in the U.S. Investment Rate: Sacrifice Times, T-Year Gains, and Investment Rate Returns. *Journal of Policy Modeling* 16, no.6 (December): 653–676.

Lewis, Kenneth A., and Laurence S. Seidman. 1996a. Conversion to a Consumption Tax, Heterogeneity, and Aggregate Saving. Department of Economics Working Paper No. 96–1, University of Delaware.

Lewis, Kenneth A., and Laurence S. Seidman. 1996b. Conversion to a Consumption Tax in a Growth Model with Heterogeneity. Department of Economics Working Paper, University of Delaware.

McCaffery, Edward J. 1994a. The Political Liberal Case against the Estate Tax. *Philosophy and Public Affairs* 23, no.4 (fall): 281–297.

McCaffery, Edward J. 1994b. The Uneasy Case for Wealth Transfer Taxation. *Yale Law Journal* 104, no.2 (November): 283–365.

McCaffery, Edward J. 1995. Rethinking the Estate Tax. *Tax Notes* (June 19): 1678–1681.

McLure, Charles E. 1987. *The Value-Added Tax.* Washington, D.C.: American Enterprise Institute.

McLure, Charles E. 1988. The 1986 Act: Tax Reform's Finest Hour or Death Throes of the Income Tax? *National Tax Journal* 41, no.3 (September): 303–315.

Mieszkowski, Peter. 1980. The Advisability and Feasibility of an Expenditure Tax System. In *The Economics of Taxation,* ed. Henry J. Aaron and Michael J. Boskin, 179–201. Washington, D.C.: Brookings Institution.

Musgrave, Richard A., and Peggy B. Musgrave. 1989. *Public Finance in Theory and Practice* (5th ed.). New York: McGraw-Hill.

Organization for Economic Cooperation and Development (OECD). 1994a. *National Accounts, 1960–1992, Main Aggregates Volume I.* Paris: OECD.

Organization for Economic Cooperation and Development (OECD). 1994b. *Taxation and Household Saving.* Paris: OECD.

Pechman, Joseph A. 1987. A Consumption Tax Is Not Desirable for the United States. In *The Consumption Tax: A Better Alternative?,* ed. Charls E. Walker and Mark A. Bloomfield, 271–274. Cambridge, MA: Ballinger.

Pechman, Joseph A. 1990. The Future of the Income Tax. *American Economic Review* 80, no.1 (March): 1–20.

Philips, Lawrence C., and John L. Cramer. 1993. *Prentice Hall's Federal Taxation, 1994, Individuals.* Englewood Cliffs, NJ: Prentice Hall.

Rosen, Harvey S. 1995. *Public Finance* (4th ed.). Chicago: Irwin.

Seidman, Laurence S. 1980. The Personal Consumption Tax and Social Welfare. *Challenge* 23, no.4 (September): 10–16.

Seidman, Laurence S. 1981. A Personal Consumption Tax: Can It Break the Capital Formation Deadlock? *Federal Reserve Bank of Philadelphia Business Review* (January): 3–9.

Seidman, Laurence S. 1983. Taxes in a Life Cycle Growth Model with Bequests and Inheritances. *American Economic Review* 73, no.3 (June): 437–441.

Seidman, Laurence S. 1984a. Conversion to a Consumption Tax: The Transition in a Life-Cycle Growth Model. *Journal of Political Economy* 92, no.2 (April): 247–267.

Seidman, Laurence S. 1984b. The Welfare Economics of Taxes: A Three-Class Disposable Income Growth Model. *Public Finance Quarterly* 12, no.1 (January): 3–26.

Seidman, Laurence S. 1987. *Macroeconomics.* San Diego: Harcourt Brace Jovanovich.

Seidman, Laurence S. 1989. Boost Saving with a Personal Consumption Tax. *Challenge* 32, no.6 (November): 44–50.

Seidman, Laurence S. 1990a. Is a Consumption Tax Equivalent to a Wage Tax? *Public Finance Quarterly* 18, no.1 (January): 65–76.

Seidman, Laurence S. 1990b. *Saving for America's Economic Future: Parables and Policies.* Armonk, NY: M.E. Sharpe.

Seidman, Laurence S. 1994a. A Better Way to Tax. *Public Interest* 114 (winter): 65–72.

Seidman, Laurence S. 1994b. Health Card: A New Prescription for National Health Insurance. *Challenge* 37, no.4 (July): 35–42.

Seidman, Laurence S. 1995. Health Card: A New Reform Plan. *Medical Group Management Journal* 42, no.4 (July): 32–34.

Seidman, Laurence S., and Kenneth A. Lewis. 1993. Increasing the Saving Rate: An Analysis of the Transition Path. In *The Economics of Saving,* ed. James H. Gapinski, 241–252. Boston: Kluwer.

Seidman, Laurence S., and Kenneth A. Lewis. 1996a. The Design of of a Tax Rule for Housing under a Personal Consumption Tax. *Public Finance Quarterly* (forthcoming).

Seidman, Laurence S., and Kenneth A. Lewis. 1996b. Transitional Protection during Conversion to a Personal Consumption Tax. Department of Economics Working Paper, University of Delaware.

Seidman, Laurence S., and Stephen B. Maurer. 1982. Taxes and Capital Intensity in a Two-Class Disposable Income Growth Model. *Journal of Public Economics* 19, no.2 (November): 243–259.

Seidman, Laurence S., and Stephen B. Maurer. 1984. The Consumption Tax, Horizontal Redistribution, and Aggregate Saving. *Mathematical Modelling* 5, no.4: 205–222.

Sheffrin, Steven M. 1993. *National Tax Journal* 46, no.3 (September): 301–308.

Simons, Henry C. 1938. *Personal Income Taxation.* Chicago: University of Chicago Press.

Steurle, Eugene. 1996. Private Pensions under a Consumption Tax. *Tax Notes* 70, no.14 (March 25): 1831–1832.

Summers, Lawrence H. 1981. Capital Taxation and Accumulation in a Life Cycle Growth Model. *American Economic Review* 71, no.4 (September): 533–544.

Summers, Lawrence H. 1984a. The After-Tax Rate of Return Affects Private Savings. *American Economic Review Papers and Proceedings* 74, no.2 (May): 249–253.

Summers, Lawrence H. 1984b. An Equity Case for Consumption Taxation. In *New Directions in Federal Tax Policy for the 1980s,* ed. Charls E. Walker and Mark A. Bloomfield, 257–260. Cambridge, MA: Ballinger.

Thurow, Lester C. 1985. *The Zero-Sum Solution.* New York: Simon and Schuster.

U.S. Treasury. 1977. *Blueprints for Basic Tax Reform.* Washington, D.C.

U.S. Treasury. 1984. *Blueprints for Basic Tax Reform* (2d ed.). Arlington, VA: Tax Analysts.

U.S. Treasury. 1984. *Tax Reform for Fairness, Simplicity, and Economic Growth.* Volume 1.

U.S. Treasury, Office of Tax Analysis. 1995. Statement of Eric Toder before the Senate Budget Committee, February 22.

U.S. Treasury, Office of Tax Analysis. 1996. New Armey-Shelby Flat Tax Would Still Lose Money. *Tax Notes* 70, no.4 (January 22): 451–461.

Venti, Steven F., and David A. Wise. 1990. Have IRA's Increased U.S. Saving?: Evidence from Consumer Expenditure Surveys. *Quarterly Journal of Economics* 105, no.3: 661–698.

Warren, Alvin C. 1975. Fairness and a Consumption-Type or Cash Flow Personal Income Tax. *Harvard Law Review* 88: 931–946.

Warren, Alvin C. 1995. The Proposal for an `Unlimited Savings Allowance.' *Tax Notes* 68, no.9 (August 28): 1103–1108.

Weidenbaum, Murray. 1996. The Nunn-Domenici USA Tax: Analysis and Comparisons. In *Frontiers of Tax Reform,* ed. Michael J. Boskin, 54–69. Stanford, CA: Hoover Institution.

Index